WELCOME TO THE WORLD OF CULINARY

This book is your guide to enchanting salad recipes that will ... flavor, and energy. Imagine a salad of tender arugula paired with the ... and crunchy nuts—or a refreshing combination of watermelon, feta, ... summer day. These dishes await you in the pages of this book. Each ... a little spell crafted for health and enjoyment, and every salad carries the essence of nature's power.

Since ancient times, our ancestors thrived on natural foods—fresh vegetables, greens, and fruits found in the wild. We evolved in harmony with these gifts, and our bodies derive the most benefits from them—boosting the immune system, improving digestion, and maintaining energy levels. Plant-based eating isn't just a trend; it's a fundamental need of our bodies, rooted in nature itself. This book invites you to return to those roots—to the food that is a part of our genetic heritage.

Today, science reveals fascinating insights into our health. Our gut is a universe of its own, where a constant battle takes place between "good" bacteria, such as lactobacilli and bifidobacteria, which support our well-being, and "bad" bacteria, like clostridia and E. coli, which can cause inflammation and illness. Salads and fresh vegetables are the best nourishment for the "good" bacteria, helping us maintain robust health, a positive mood, and a long life. Every plate of salad, therefore, is a contribution to your body's balance and harmony.

Each season brings its own changes in nature, along with unique treasures that can become the foundation of our meals. In spring—delicate arugula and crisp radishes; in summer—juicy berries and cooling cucumbers; in autumn—sweet pumpkin and crunchy beets; and in winter—vibrant oranges and aromatic spices. In this book, you'll uncover the magic of every season, and together, we'll learn how to harness it to create dishes that will fill your life with flavor and joy.

P.S.
If you enjoy this book or find a favorite recipe — please take a moment to scan the QR code at the end and leave a review. Your feedback helps others discover healthy and flavorful cooking — and inspires me to keep sharing more!

Table of Contents

INTRODUCTION: THE MAGIC OF SEASONS IN YOUR KITCHEN 6
QUICK GUIDE TO SELECTING AND PREPARING INGREDIENTS 6
SALAD BUILDER – HOW TO CREATE THE PERFECT FLAVOR BALANCE 7
FLAVOR MAGIC - CRAFTING THE ULTIMATE SALAD DRESSINGS 9
SEASONAL INGREDIENTS FOR EVERY TIME OF YEAR 10
MICROBIOTA AND GUT HEALTH 11

SPRING MAGIC: SALADS THAT AWAKEN THE SENSES 12
SPRING FRESHNESS: LIGHT SALAD WITH BABY GREENS AND RADISH 13
BRIGHT SPRING DAY: SPINACH SALAD WITH STRAWBERRIES AND ALMONDS 13
CRISP FRESHNESS: SALAD WITH BABY PEAS AND MINT 14
SPRING AROMA: SALAD WITH ARUGULA, RADISH, AND AVOCADO 14
AWAKENING OF NATURE: SALAD WITH GREEN ONIONS AND FRESH SPROUTS 15
COZY COMFORT: WARM SALAD WITH BABY POTATOES AND GREEN ONIONS 15
FIRST RAY OF SUNSHINE: ASPARAGUS AND LEMON DRESSING SALAD 16
CRISP SPRING: SALAD WITH RADISH, GREEN APPLE, AND DILL 16
SPRING ABUNDANCE: SALAD WITH BROCCOLI, ALMONDS, AND DRIED CRANBERRIES 17
CITRUS FRESHNESS: SALAD WITH BABY SPINACH, GRAPEFRUIT, AND WALNUTS 17
NATURE'S INSPIRATION: SALAD WITH SPRING HERBS AND PINE NUTS 18
TENDER GREENS: SALAD WITH BABY ASPARAGUS, PEAS, AND MINT DRESSING 18

SUMMER SALADS: FRESHNESS AND THE ABUNDANCE OF SUNNY FLAVORS 19
SUMMER DELIGHT: SALAD WITH WATERMELON, FETA, AND MINT 20
ITALIAN CLASSIC: CAPRESE WITH TOMATOES AND FRESH BASIL 20
GARDEN COOL: REFRESHING CUCUMBER SALAD WITH YOGURT AND DILL 21
SUMMER ABUNDANCE: SALAD WITH CORN, AVOCADO, AND CHERRY TOMATOES 21
BERRY MAGIC: SALAD WITH BLUEBERRIES, RASPBERRIES, AND ARUGULA 22
TROPICAL BREEZE: SALAD WITH MANGO AND CILANTRO 22
SWEET SUMMER EVENING: SALAD WITH PEACHES, MOZZARELLA, AND BASIL 23
MEDITERRANEAN LIGHTNESS: SUMMER SALAD WITH PASTA, OLIVES, AND CHERRY TOMATOES 23
ASIAN HARMONY: SALAD WITH RED CABBAGE, CARROTS, AND SESAME DRESSING 24
SUMMER SPARK: SALAD WITH SHRIMP, PINEAPPLE, AND CHILI 24
SUMMER GARDEN: SALAD WITH TOMATOES, CUCUMBERS, AND BELL PEPPERS 25
FRUITY BLAST: SALAD WITH PINEAPPLE, KIWI, AND FRESH MINT 25

AUTUMN SYMPHONY: WARMTH AND FLAVOR OF THE GOLDEN SEASON 26
AUTUMN HARMONY: WARM SALAD WITH PUMPKIN, BEETS, AND GOAT CHEESE 27
VELVET EVENING: COUSCOUS SALAD WITH POMEGRANATE AND PINE NUTS 27
SWEET AUTUMN: ROASTED CARROT SALAD WITH HONEY AND PECANS 28
AUTUMN DELIGHT: APPLE SALAD WITH WALNUTS AND MAPLE SYRUP 28
CRUNCHY COMFORT: CABBAGE SALAD WITH TOASTED SEEDS 29

AUTUMN FLAME: ROASTED BRUSSELS SPROUT AND BACON SALAD 29
PUMPKIN INSPIRATION: ROASTED PUMPKIN AND QUINOA SALAD 30
FOREST FLAVOR: SAUTÉED MUSHROOM AND ARUGULA SALAD 30
ELEGANT AUTUMN: PEAR, WALNUT, AND BLUE CHEESE SALAD..31
ROOT POWER: SALAD WITH ROOT VEGETABLES AND VINAIGRETTE 31
WARM DELIGHT: LENTIL, SPINACH, AND ROASTED VEGETABLE SALAD 32
HARVEST INSPIRATION: WARM SALAD WITH SAUTÉED APPLES, SPINACH, AND PECANS 32

WINTER SALADS: WARMTH AND WINTER'S STRENGTH 33

WINTER FRESHNESS — SALAD WITH CITRUS AND POMEGRANATE 34
WINTER WARMTH — ROASTED ROOT VEGETABLE SALAD WITH SPICES 34
WINTER CRUNCH — CABBAGE AND CARROT SALAD WITH SESAME DRESSING 35
CITRUS DELIGHT — SALAD WITH ORANGE, FENNEL, AND WALNUTS 35
FESTIVE CHEER — SALAD WITH CRANBERRIES, SPINACH, AND FETA CHEESE 36
WARM COMFORT — SALAD WITH POTATOES, GARLIC, AND ROSEMARY 36
WINTER VIOLET — SALAD WITH RED CABBAGE AND APPLE CIDER VINEGAR 37
WARM TENDERNESS — SALAD WITH ROASTED SWEET POTATO AND AVOCADO 37
WINTER RICHES — SALAD WITH ROASTED ROOT VEGETABLES AND POMEGRANATE 38
CRUNCHY WINTER — SALAD WITH PUMPKIN SEEDS AND GREEN CABBAGE 38
WINTER FOREST WONDER — SALAD WITH PICKLED MUSHROOMS AND ONIONS 39
WINTER FANTASY — ROASTED BEET AND GOAT CHEESE SALAD 39

FESTIVE SALADS FOR SPECIAL OCCASIONS: MAGIC ON YOUR TABLE 40

CHRISTMAS TALE — SALAD WITH RED CABBAGE AND APPLES 41
FESTIVE DELIGHT — SALAD WITH CARAMELIZED NUTS AND GRAPES 41
NEW YEAR'S SURPRISE — SALAD WITH AVOCADO AND SHRIMP 42
SOPHISTICATED CELEBRATION — SALAD WITH GOAT CHEESE AND FIGS 42
ENCHANTED EVENING — HOLIDAY SALAD WITH ROASTED PEAR AND BLUE CHEESE 43
SUNNY DELIGHT — SALAD WITH HALLOUMI CHEESE AND GRILLED PEACHES 43
CITRUS DUCK — SALAD WITH SMOKED DUCK AND ORANGES 44
TROPICAL FRESHNESS — SALAD WITH GRAPEFRUIT, AVOCADO, AND ARUGULA 44
BERRY TENDERNESS — SALAD WITH GRILLED CHICKEN AND RASPBERRIES 45
EASTERN TALE — SALAD WITH DATES, ALMONDS, AND YOGURT DRESSING 45
FESTIVE GLOW — SALAD WITH GRAPES, NUTS, AND BRIE CHEESE 46
CHRISTMAS MIRACLE — SALAD WITH MANDARINS, WALNUTS, AND YOGURT DRESSING 46

PROTEIN SALADS: POWER AND ENERGY FOR AN ACTIVE LIFE 47

CITRUS BOOST — SALAD WITH CHICKEN, AVOCADO, AND GRAPEFRUIT 48
SEA BREEZE — TUNA WITH BEANS AND FRESH GREENS 48
PROTEIN HARMONY — QUINOA, EGG, AND CHICKPEA SALAD 49
CRANBERRY DELIGHT — TURKEY SALAD WITH CRANBERRY SAUCE 49
SEA FRESHNESS — SHRIMP AND AVOCADO SALAD 50
TERIYAKI INSPIRATION — BEEF SALAD WITH TERIYAKI SAUCE 50

HOMELY COMFORT — BUCKWHEAT, EGG, AND HERB SALAD 51
PROTEIN DELICACY — CHICKEN, BROCCOLI, AND ALMOND SALAD 51
CITRUS SALMON — SALAD WITH SALMON AND ORANGE SAUCE 52
ENERGY GREENS — SALAD WITH LENTILS, EGG, AND SPINACH 52
SPICY TOUCH — SALAD WITH ROAST BEEF AND HORSERADISH DRESSING 53
GREEK INSPIRATION — SALAD WITH CHICKEN, FETA, AND OLIVES 53

VEGAN SALADS: HARMONY WITH NATURE AND PURE FLAVORS 54

NATURAL ENERGY— CHICKPEA AND FRESH VEGETABLE SALAD 55
MEDITERRANEAN INSPIRATION — TABOULI WITH HERBS AND LEMON 55
LEMON FRESHNESS – QUINOA SALAD WITH AVOCADO AND LEMON DRESSING 56
VEGETABLE WARMTH – ROASTED VEGETABLE SALAD WITH TAHINI 56
TOFU AND GREENS – LIGHTNESS AND FRESHNESS 57
SEA INSPIRATION – SEAWEED SALAD WITH SESAME DRESSING 57
BEETROOT DELIGHT – ROASTED BEET SALAD WITH WALNUTS 58
POMEGRANATE FRESHNESS – QUINOA, SPINACH, AND POMEGRANATE SALAD 58
EASTERN CHARM – EGGPLANT AND TAHINI SALAD 59
SPICY PUMPKIN – CHICKPEA AND CORIANDER SALAD 59
GREEN FRESHNESS – CUCUMBER, AVOCADO, AND GREEN ONION SALAD 60
WARM CHICKPEA – CHICKPEA, SPINACH, AND ROASTED VEGETABLE SALAD 60

LIGHT SALADS FOR EVERY DAY: FRESHNESS AND EASE IN ANY SEASON 61

TOMATO DELIGHT — LIGHT TOMATO AND BASIL SALAD 62
CRUNCHY FRESHNESS — YOUNG CABBAGE SALAD WITH APPLE 63
SWEET CRUNCH — CARROT SALAD WITH RAISINS AND NUTS 63
SPRING LIGHTNESS — RADISH SALAD WITH SOUR CREAM AND GREEN ONION 64
CITRUS INSPIRATION — FRESH SPINACH SALAD WITH EGG AND LEMON DRESSING 64
SUMMER CRUNCH — GREEN BEAN AND CHERRY TOMATO SALAD 65
ITALIAN SIMPLICITY — ARUGULA, PARMESAN, AND LEMON DRESSING SALAD 65
REFRESHING SIMPLICITY — CABBAGE, CARROT, AND APPLE CIDER VINEGAR SALAD 66
MEDITERRANEAN BREEZE — CUCUMBER, MINT, AND FETA SALAD 66
SUMMER INSPIRATION — ZUCCHINI SALAD WITH LEMON OIL 67
LIGHT SPRING MIX — SALAD WITH GREEN PEAS, RADISH, AND MINT DRESSING 67

ELIXIRS OF FLAVOR: THE MAGIC OF SALAD DRESSINGS 68

Health in Every Drop 68
Flavor Transformation: The Alchemy of Dressings 68
GOLDEN VINAIGRETTE 69
MEDITERRANEAN LEMON BASIL DRESSING 69
GARLIC LEMON YOGURT DRESSING 70
ASIAN SESAME GINGER DRESSING 70
CREAMY AVOCADO LIME DRESSING 71
NUTTY MAPLE DRESSING 71

CITRUS MINT DRESSING	72
HONEY MUSTARD BALSAMIC DRESSING	72
SPINACH GARLIC DRESSING	73
SPINACH GARLIC DRESSING	73

CONCLUSION 74

INTRODUCTION: THE MAGIC OF SEASONS IN YOUR KITCHEN

QUICK GUIDE TO SELECTING AND PREPARING INGREDIENTS

At the heart of every magical salad lie fresh and high-quality ingredients. Choosing, storing, and preparing these products are crucial steps in the enchanting process that makes your dishes both delicious and nutritious. Let's explore how to make the most of simple ingredients to create inspired meals.

THE MAGIC OF FRESH INGREDIENTS

Fresh vegetables and fruits are a true treasure trove of health. Packed with vitamins, minerals, and antioxidants, they help strengthen immunity, sustain energy, and combat inflammation. Seasonal produce, imbued with the power of nature, becomes the key to creating salads brimming with vibrant flavors and colors.

SECRETS TO CHOOSING INGREDIENTS

Choosing the right ingredients is the first step in your culinary spell:

- **Color and Aroma:** Vegetables and fruits at their peak ripeness boast rich colors and natural fragrances. Ripe tomatoes are bright red and fragrant, peaches are slightly soft and aromatic, and pineapples exude a sweet smell and have a slightly yielding skin.
- **Texture:** Fresh produce is always firm and juicy. Avoid wilted greens or soft, dull vegetables.

HOW TO PRESERVE INGREDIENT FRESHNESS

Extend the life of your ingredients with these tips:

- **Greens:** Wrap in a slightly damp towel and store in the refrigerator. This keeps them crisp and fresh.
- **Vegetables and Fruits:** Store in a cool place, but not all in the fridge. For example, tomatoes retain their flavor better at room temperature.
- **Containers:** Place chopped vegetables in airtight or vacuum-sealed containers to keep them fresh for several days.

EASE OF PREPARATION AND PRESENTATION

- **Prepare Ahead:** Chop vegetables and store them in containers to speed up the cooking process.
- **Color Magic:** Create a bright palette by mixing green spinach leaves, red tomatoes, yellow bell peppers, and purple onions. Such a salad will be not only delicious but also visually stunning.
- **Finishing Touches:** Add a pinch of seeds or edible flowers to complete the dish. These small details make the salad both flavorful and magically appealing.

Remember, the magic of salads starts with your hands. Choose the best ingredients and handle them with love and care—and each dish will become your personal culinary spell!

SALAD BUILDER – HOW TO CREATE THE PERFECT FLAVOR BALANCE

The magic of an ideal salad lies in its harmonious taste that delights and surprises. This section will help you master the art of balancing key flavors so every salad becomes a culinary masterpiece.

THE FIVE KEY FLAVORS: THE FOUNDATION OF BALANCE

Each flavor plays its role, adding depth and complexity to a dish:

- **Sweet:** Adds softness and completeness.
  Examples: honey, maple syrup, sweet fruits (berries, mango), roasted vegetables (carrots, pumpkin).
- **Salty:** Enhances the flavors of other ingredients.
  Examples: sea salt, cheese (feta, parmesan), olives, capers.
- **Sour:** Refreshes and brightens the dish.
  Examples: lemon juice, vinegar (apple cider, balsamic), citrus fruits (orange, grapefruit).
- **Bitter:** Adds sophistication and intriguing depth.
  Examples: arugula, endive, grapefruit, cocoa.
- **Umami:** The "savory richness" that completes the flavor profile.
  Examples: mushrooms, soy sauce, tomatoes, parmesan cheese.

Tip: Play with proportions. For example, in a summer salad, add a drop of sweet honey, a touch of lemon's acidity, and a hint of saltiness through olives.

GUIDE TO COMBINING FLAVORS

- **Sweet + Sour:** Grapes and feta cheese with a light vinegar dressing—a classic combination.
- **Salty + Umami:** Roasted mushrooms with goat cheese and olives.
- **Bitter + Sweet:** Arugula with caramelized pear and nuts.
- **Sour + Umami:** Roasted tomatoes with basil and lemon dressing.

IDEAS FOR MULTI-LAYERED SALADS

Building layers helps enhance flavor balance:

- **Base:** Fresh greens or grains (arugula, quinoa, bulgur).
- **Main Flavor:** A protein element (chicken, tofu, eggs).
- **Bright Accent:** Fruits, berries, or pickled vegetables.
- **Textural Element:** Nuts, seeds, croutons.
- **Dressing:** The finishing touch to tie the flavors together.

BALANCE THROUGH TEXTURES

Sometimes flavor balance is achieved through textural contrasts:

- **Crunchy (nuts, seeds) + Creamy (avocado, yogurt).**
- **Juicy (citrus, berries) + Dense (grains, roasted vegetables).**

Tip: Use spices and herbs to enhance flavors. For example, cilantro for freshness or paprika for sweetness.

HOW TO AVOID IMBALANCE

- **Too sour:** Add a bit of honey or sweet fruit.
- **Too salty:** Balance with greens or soft textures like avocado.
- **Lacking richness:** Add umami elements like mushrooms or parmesan.

PRACTICAL EXERCISE: YOUR FIRST PERFECTLY BALANCED SALAD

Example recipe:

- **Base:** A mix of arugula and spinach.
- **Main Flavor:** Roasted pumpkin.
- **Bright Accent:** Pomegranate seeds.
- **Textural Element:** Toasted almonds.
- **Dressing:** A blend of olive oil, lemon juice, and a pinch of honey.

Why does this work?
The sweetness of pumpkin balances the acidity of lemon and pomegranate, while the bitterness of arugula and the crunch of almonds add textural and flavor depth.

BALANCE FOR DIFFERENT SEASONS

Each season brings its unique flavors:

- **Spring:** Freshness and tanginess (lemon, herbs, green vegetables).
- **Summer:** Lightness and sweetness (fruits, berries, cucumbers).
- **Autumn:** Comfort and richness (pumpkin, nuts, grains).
- **Winter:** Warmth and contrasts (citrus fruits, root vegetables, spices).

Creating the perfect flavor balance is an art that inspires and captivates. A salad can be a light meal or a magical spell for the soul and body. Experiment with these tips, and every salad you make will be perfect!

FLAVOR MAGIC - CRAFTING THE ULTIMATE SALAD DRESSINGS

A dressing is the finishing touch that unites the ingredients of a salad and gives the dish its unique character. The magic of a dressing lies in its balance, texture, and aroma. Discover how to craft the perfect dressing that will transform your salad into a culinary masterpiece.

THE 3:1 PRINCIPLE — THE FOUNDATION OF HARMONY

For a classic dressing, rely on the tried-and-true ratio:

- **3 parts oil** (olive, nut, or even sesame oil) to **1 part acid** (vinegar, lemon, or lime juice).

This ratio creates the softness of the oil and the brightness of the acid, ensuring a perfect flavor balance.
Tip: If you prefer a more tangy flavor, adjust the ratio to 2:1, allowing the acidity to shine a bit more.

EMULSIFIERS — THE MAGIC OF TEXTURE

To achieve a smooth and even dressing, include ingredients that help blend oil and acid:

- **Dijon mustard:** Adds a slight tanginess.
- **Honey:** Provides softness and a touch of sweetness.

Emulsifiers not only improve texture but also help the dressing coat each salad ingredient evenly.

PLAYING WITH AROMAS AND ACCENTS

Give your dressing a unique personality by adding aromatic elements:

- **Fresh herbs:** Basil, cilantro, dill, or parsley bring freshness.
- **Spices:** Black pepper, smoked paprika, coriander, or cumin add depth of flavor.
- **Garlic:** For a touch of spiciness and aroma.

Tip: Try adding lemon or orange zest for a citrusy accent that makes the dressing truly magical.

HOW TO MAKE A MAGICAL DRESSING

1. Mix oil and acid in the proper ratio.
2. Add an emulsifier to create a smooth texture.
3. Incorporate aromatic accents—herbs, spices, or zest.
4. Shake everything in a jar or whisk until smooth.

YOUR DRESSING, YOUR MAGIC

The perfect dressing is a reflection of your taste and mood. Experiment, try new combinations, and create your own culinary spells. Let every dressing make your salad unforgettable!

SEASONAL INGREDIENTS FOR EVERY TIME OF YEAR

Each season reveals its unique gifts of nature, offering fresh ingredients brimming with flavor and nutrients. Choosing seasonal products not only enhances the taste of your dishes but also helps you stay in harmony with nature. Let's dive into the basket of each season and discover the magic of its aromas.

SPRING: AWAKENING FLAVORS

Spring brings freshness and lightness, reminding us of new beginnings. It's the season for tender greens and the first vegetables that awaken the taste buds.

- **What to use:** Baby spinach, arugula, green onions, radishes.
- **Salad idea:** Spinach salad with radishes, eggs, and a light lemon dressing.
  Tip: Add edible flowers, such as nasturtium, to give your salad a spring accent.

SUMMER: ABUNDANCE OF FRESHNESS

Summer is a burst of colors, aromas, and flavors. The produce of this season is rich in water, making it perfect for refreshing and light salads.

- **What to use:** Tomatoes, cucumbers, berries, watermelon, fresh herbs.
- **Salad idea:** Watermelon, feta, and mint salad.
  Tip: Use frozen berries or cucumber juice cubes to add a cooling effect to your salad on a hot day.

AUTUMN: WARMTH AND RICHNESS

Autumn is all about coziness and deep flavors. This is the time for hearty and warm ingredients that provide comfort and create a homey atmosphere.

- **What to use:** Pumpkin, beets, carrots, apples.
- **Salad idea:** Roasted pumpkin with pecans and feta cheese.
  Tip: Use warm spices like cinnamon or nutmeg to enhance the autumn mood.

WINTER: VIBRANCY AND VITAMINS

Winter delights us with bold and vibrant flavors that nourish the body during the colder months. It's the season of citrus fruits and nutrient-packed root vegetables.

- **What to use:** Citrus fruits, cabbage, pomegranates, root vegetables.
- **Salad idea:** Orange, pomegranate, and finely sliced cabbage salad.
  Tip: Add a warm dressing made with honey and mustard to create a contrast with the cold ingredients.

CELEBRATING THE SEASONS

Each season is a new opportunity to explore flavors, enjoy the gifts of nature, and add magic to your dishes. Let your salads reflect the beauty and diversity of the seasons!

MICROBIOTA AND GUT HEALTH

The microbiota is a hidden world within your body, playing a crucial role in maintaining health and well-being. Beneficial gut bacteria not only aid digestion but also boost immunity, sustain energy levels, and even influence mood. Carefully chosen salad ingredients can serve as true "fuel" for these tiny helpers.

PREBIOTICS AND PROBIOTICS: FOOD FOR YOUR MICROBIOTA

Some ingredients have the magical ability to support microbiota health by serving as nourishment for beneficial bacteria. These foods are rich in prebiotics—the natural "elixirs" for your gut.

- **What to use:** Onions, garlic, asparagus, bananas.
- **Salad idea:** Add thinly sliced garlic to fresh vegetables or use asparagus in warm salads.
  Tip: Experiment with fermented foods like sauerkraut or yogurt to add probiotics, which directly enrich your microbiota.

FIBER: THE KEY TO A HEALTHY GUT

Fiber is nature's gift to your body. It not only improves digestion but also creates a favorable environment for the growth of beneficial bacteria.

- **What to use:** Leafy greens, whole grains, legumes.
- **Salad idea:** Try a salad with quinoa, arugula, and roasted chickpeas.
  Tip: Use a variety of greens to maximize fiber content and enhance the dish's texture.

THE MAGIC OF HEALTH IN EVERY BOWL

When you prepare salads, you're not just making food—you're nurturing your microbiota, and thus, your overall well-being. Each ingredient becomes part of your personal spell for health and vitality.

- **Light recipe for inspiration:**
    - **Base:** Spinach and arugula.
    - **Accent:** Steamed asparagus and thinly sliced banana.
    - **Final touch:** A dressing of olive oil, lemon juice, and a hint of garlic.
      Tip: Serve the salad with a sprinkle of nuts or seeds to complete the texture and flavor profile.

Let every salad you create become a small spell, bringing health, lightness, and joy. Be inspired, experiment, and uncover the magic in every bowl!

SPRING MAGIC: SALADS THAT AWAKEN THE SENSES

Spring is a time of nature's awakening, when every leaf and flower bursts with life and energy. This chapter will inspire you to create light and refreshing dishes filled with vibrant aromas and textures. Spring salads are a delightful combination of freshness and crunch, delivering vitamins and joy to your body. Each recipe is a little spell of springtime lightness, offering energy and health. Let these salads become a source of inspiration and happiness on your table!

Spring is the season of renewal and freshness, as nature comes alive with colors and vitality. With the arrival of warmth, there's a desire for lighter, healthier meals to boost your energy. Our spring salads will help you embrace the season with ease and optimism.

The focus of spring salads is on fresh, seasonal ingredients. Crisp cucumbers, tender greens, fragrant herbs, and vitamin-rich radishes make their appearance in springtime. Fresh greens like spinach, arugula, and green onions help detoxify the body and strengthen immunity. Spring vegetables are packed with antioxidants that support youthful skin and protect overall health.

The recipes in this section bring a variety of textures and flavors—crunchy, juicy, slightly sweet, and tangy elements. For instance, the combination of radish, carrot, and apple creates a perfect balance of flavor and freshness. This chapter offers ideas for vibrant and delicious spring meals.

Spring salads can easily be adapted to suit any taste. Adding protein like eggs, cheese, or nuts can make the dish more filling. These light meals help maintain balance, improve metabolism, and support a healthy weight. Natural spring ingredients also boost immunity and enhance well-being.

Dressings for spring salads should be light and refreshing. The recipes in this chapter feature simple dressings that enhance natural flavors: lemon-based, yogurt-based, or honey and herb combinations. Lemon juice, olive oil, and mustard add a tangy twist that makes every salad irresistible.

Spring salads are a way to feel connected with nature and enjoy its gifts. They inspire and make every meal a celebration of health and taste. We've included recipes for everyday lunches and special occasions to delight your loved ones with fresh and original dishes.

Welcome to the world of spring salads! Let these recipes inspire you and bring freshness and lightness to your table. We hope each one will earn a spot in your collection of favorite dishes.

SPRING FRESHNESS: LIGHT SALAD WITH BABY GREENS AND RADISH

DESCRIPTION: This salad brings nature's awakening right to your table. Crisp radishes, tender baby greens, and a light lemon dressing create a harmonious blend of freshness and vibrancy. It's a perfect choice for those seeking lightness and inspiration in every bite—a wonderful option for a spring lunch or dinner that energizes and delights!

INGREDIENTS:
- 1 bunch of radishes (about 150 g)
- 3 1/2 oz (100 g) baby greens mix (arugula, spinach, watercress)
- 2 tbsp (30 ml) olive oil
- 1 tbsp (15 ml) lemon juice
- 1 tsp (5 ml) honey
- Pinch of salt and freshly ground pepper
- A few sprigs of dill for garnish

COOKING TIME: 10 minutes
INSTRUCTIONS:
1. Wash the radishes and slice them into thin rounds.
2. Wash and dry the baby greens thoroughly.
3. In a small bowl, mix olive oil, lemon juice, honey, salt, and pepper to prepare the dressing.
4. In a salad bowl, combine sliced radishes and greens. Drizzle with the dressing and gently toss.
5. Garnish with dill sprigs before serving.

NUTRITION (PER 100 G): 45 kcal, 1 g protein, 4 g fat, 3 g carbs, 2 g fiber.
GARNISHING TIP: For an extra touch, sprinkle some lemon zest to enhance the citrusy aroma.

BRIGHT SPRING DAY: SPINACH SALAD WITH STRAWBERRIES AND ALMONDS

DESCRIPTION: This salad is a true ode to spring. The delicate freshness of spinach meets the sweetness of juicy strawberries, while crunchy almonds add texture and richness. A light lemon and honey dressing brings the dish to life with bright citrusy notes, making it a perfect choice for a light lunch or dinner filled with springtime inspiration and magic.

INGREDIENTS:
- 3 1/2 oz (100 g) fresh spinach
- 1 cup (150 g) sliced strawberries
- 1/4 cup (30 g) almonds, lightly toasted
- 2 tbsp (30 ml) olive oil
- 1 tbsp (15 ml) lemon juice
- 1 tsp (5 ml) honey
- Pinch of salt and freshly ground pepper

COOKING TIME: 10 minutes
INSTRUCTIONS:
1. Wash and dry the spinach thoroughly.
2. Slice the strawberries thinly.
3. Lightly toast the almonds in a dry skillet until golden brown.
4. In a small bowl, mix olive oil, lemon juice, honey, salt, and pepper to prepare the dressing.
5. In a salad bowl, combine spinach, strawberries, and almonds. Drizzle with the dressing and gently toss.

NUTRITION (PER 100 G): 75 kcal, 2 g protein, 5 g fat, 6 g carbs, 2 g fiber.
GARNISHING TIP: Add a few whole strawberries or sprinkle the salad with edible flower petals for a decorative touch.

CRISP FRESHNESS: SALAD WITH BABY PEAS AND MINT

DESCRIPTION: This salad is like a breath of spring air: the sweetness of baby peas, the delicate aroma of fresh mint, and the crispness of mixed greens come together in perfect harmony of flavors and textures. A light dressing of lemon juice and olive oil enhances the natural aromas, making this dish an ideal choice for a light and inspiring lunch.

INGREDIENTS:
- 1 cup (150 g) fresh or frozen baby peas
- 3 1/2 oz (100 g) mixed salad greens
- 1/4 cup (30 g) fresh mint leaves
- 2 tbsp (30 ml) olive oil
- 1 tbsp (15 ml) lemon juice
- Pinch of salt and freshly ground pepper
- A few lemon slices for garnish

COOKING TIME: 10 minutes

INSTRUCTIONS:
1. If using frozen peas, thaw them in hot water for 1–2 minutes, then rinse with cold water and pat dry.
2. Wash and dry the salad greens and mint leaves.
3. In a small bowl, whisk together olive oil, lemon juice, salt, and pepper to prepare the dressing.
4. In a salad bowl, combine the greens, peas, and mint. Drizzle with the dressing and gently toss.
5. Garnish with lemon slices before serving.

NUTRITION (PER 100 G): 70 kcal, 2 g protein, 5 g fat, 4 g carbs, 2 g fiber.

GARNISHING TIP: For an elegant touch, sprinkle some grated lemon zest or add a few mint sprigs on top of the salad.

SPRING AROMA: SALAD WITH ARUGULA, RADISH, AND AVOCADO

DESCRIPTION: This salad combines the crispness of radish, the zesty freshness of arugula, and the creaminess of avocado to create a harmonious dish bursting with vibrant spring flavors. A light lemon dressing enhances the natural aromas, making this salad the perfect choice for a light lunch or dinner that energizes and inspires.

INGREDIENTS:
- 1 bunch of radishes (about 150 g)
- 1 ripe avocado
- 3 1/2 oz (100 g) arugula
- 2 tbsp (30 ml) olive oil
- 1 tbsp (15 ml) lemon juice
- Pinch of salt and freshly ground pepper
- A few lemon slices for garnish

COOKING TIME: 10 minutes

INSTRUCTIONS:
1. Wash the radishes and slice them into thin rounds.
2. Cut the avocado into slices or cubes.
3. Wash and dry the arugula.
4. In a small bowl, mix olive oil, lemon juice, salt, and pepper to prepare the dressing.
5. In a salad bowl, combine the radishes, avocado, and arugula. Drizzle with the dressing and gently toss.
6. Garnish the salad with lemon slices before serving.

NUTRITION (PER 100 G): 95 kcal, 2 g protein, 8 g fat, 5 g carbs, 3 g fiber.

GARNISHING TIP: For a visually appealing presentation, add a few thin slices of radish and avocado on top of the salad.

AWAKENING OF NATURE: SALAD WITH GREEN ONIONS AND FRESH SPROUTS

DESCRIPTION: This salad brings a plateful of springtime vibes with the freshness of green onions and the crispness of tender sprouts. A light olive oil dressing with bright lemon notes highlights the natural aromas, making this dish a perfect addition to any lunch or dinner.

INGREDIENTS:
- 1 bunch of green onions (about 50 g)
- 1 cup (150 g) fresh sprouts (alfalfa, pea shoots, or watercress)
- 3 1/2 oz (100 g) spring greens mix
- 2 tbsp (30 ml) olive oil
- 1 tbsp (15 ml) lemon juice
- Pinch of salt and freshly ground pepper

COOKING TIME: 10 minutes

INSTRUCTIONS:
1. Wash the green onions and slice them into thin rings.
2. Rinse and pat dry the fresh sprouts.
3. Wash and dry the spring greens mix.
4. In a small bowl, whisk together olive oil, lemon juice, salt, and pepper to prepare the dressing.
5. In a salad bowl, combine the greens, green onions, and sprouts. Drizzle with the dressing and gently toss.
6. Serve the salad immediately and enjoy its fresh spring flavors.

NUTRITION (PER 100 G): 60 kcal, 2 g protein, 4 g fat, 4 g carbs, 2 g fiber.

GARNISHING TIP: For added texture, sprinkle the salad with a small amount of sesame seeds or garnish with a lemon wedge on the side.

COZY COMFORT: WARM SALAD WITH BABY POTATOES AND GREEN ONIONS

DESCRIPTION: This warm salad combines the tender texture of baby potatoes with the fresh aroma of green onions. A light mustard-honey dressing adds depth and richness to the dish, making it an ideal choice for a cozy family dinner filled with warmth and flavor.

INGREDIENTS:
- 1 lb (450 g) baby potatoes
- 1/4 cup (30 g) chopped green onions
- 2 tbsp (30 ml) olive oil
- 1 tbsp (15 ml) Dijon mustard
- 1 tsp (5 ml) honey
- 1 tbsp (15 ml) apple cider vinegar
- Pinch of salt and freshly ground pepper

COOKING TIME: Prep: 15 minutes, Cook: 15 minutes

INSTRUCTIONS:
1. Thoroughly wash the baby potatoes and boil them in salted water until tender (15–20 minutes). Let cool slightly, then cut into halves or quarters.
2. Chop the green onions into small rings.
3. In a small bowl, mix olive oil, mustard, honey, vinegar, salt, and pepper to prepare the dressing.
4. In a salad bowl, combine the warm potatoes and green onions. Drizzle with the dressing and gently toss.
5. Serve the salad warm for the best flavor experience.

NUTRITION (PER 100 G): 110 kcal, 2 g protein, 4 g fat, 16 g carbs, 2 g fiber.

GARNISHING TIP: Top with fresh dill sprigs or sprinkle with lightly toasted sesame seeds for added aroma and visual appeal.

FIRST RAY OF SUNSHINE: ASPARAGUS AND LEMON DRESSING SALAD

DESCRIPTION: This salad combines the freshness of tender asparagus shoots, the delicacy of young greens, and the tangy notes of a lemon dressing. Light and elegant, this dish is a perfect choice for a spring lunch or dinner, bringing freshness and grace to your table.

INGREDIENTS:
- 1/2 bunch (150 g) fresh green asparagus
- 3 1/2 oz (100 g) mixed salad greens (arugula, spinach)
- 2 tbsp (30 ml) olive oil
- 1 tbsp (15 ml) lemon juice
- 1 tsp (5 ml) honey
- Pinch of salt and freshly ground pepper
- A few lemon slices for garnish

COOKING TIME: Prep: 10 minutes, Cook: 3 minutes

INSTRUCTIONS:
1. Wash the asparagus, trim the tough ends, and blanch the spears in salted water for 2–3 minutes. Immediately rinse with cold water to preserve the vibrant color and pat dry.
2. Wash and dry the salad greens thoroughly.
3. In a small bowl, whisk together olive oil, lemon juice, honey, salt, and pepper to prepare the dressing.
4. Arrange the greens and asparagus on a serving plate, drizzle with the dressing, and gently toss.
5. Garnish with lemon slices before serving.

NUTRITION (PER 100 G): 70 kcal, 2 g protein, 5 g fat, 5 g carbs, 2 g fiber.

GARNISHING TIP: For added sophistication, sprinkle with grated lemon zest or a few black sesame seeds for contrast and elegance.

CRISP SPRING: SALAD WITH RADISH, GREEN APPLE, AND DILL

DESCRIPTION: This salad combines the freshness of green apple, the crunchy texture of radish, and the aromatic hint of dill. A light lemon juice dressing highlights the natural flavors, creating a perfect dish for a spring lunch that delights with its simplicity and elegance.

INGREDIENTS:
- 1 bunch of radishes (about 150 g)
- 1 medium green apple (about 200 g)
- 3 1/2 oz (100 g) mixed salad greens
- 2 tbsp (30 ml) olive oil
- 1 tbsp (15 ml) lemon juice
- Pinch of salt and freshly ground pepper
- 2 sprigs of fresh dill

COOKING TIME: 10 minutes

INSTRUCTIONS:
1. Wash the radishes and slice them into thin rounds.
2. Peel the green apple and cut it into thin slices or matchsticks.
3. Wash and dry the salad greens thoroughly.
4. In a small bowl, mix olive oil, lemon juice, salt, and pepper to prepare the dressing.
5. In a salad bowl, combine the radishes, apple, greens, and dill. Drizzle with the dressing and gently toss.
6. Serve immediately to preserve the freshness and crunchiness of the ingredients.

NUTRITION (PER 100 G): 65 kcal, 1 g protein, 4 g fat, 6 g carbs, 2 g fiber.

GARNISHING TIP: Add a few apple slices and dill sprigs on top of the salad for a decorative touch.

SPRING ABUNDANCE: SALAD WITH BROCCOLI, ALMONDS, AND DRIED CRANBERRIES

DESCRIPTION: This salad combines the crunchy texture of broccoli, the sweet notes of dried cranberries, and the nutty depth of roasted almonds. A light honey-mustard dressing ties these elements together in perfect harmony, making the dish both nutritious and vibrant—ideal for any lunch or dinner.

INGREDIENTS:

- 2 cups (300 g) fresh broccoli florets
- 1/4 cup (30 g) sliced almonds, lightly toasted
- 1/4 cup (30 g) dried cranberries
- 3 1/2 oz (100 g) mixed salad greens
- 2 tbsp (30 ml) olive oil
- 1 tbsp (15 ml) apple cider vinegar
- 1 tsp (5 ml) honey
- 1 tsp (5 ml) Dijon mustard
- Pinch of salt and freshly ground pepper

COOKING TIME: 15 minutes

INSTRUCTIONS:
1. Wash the broccoli and cut the florets into small pieces. Blanch in salted boiling water for 2 minutes, then rinse with cold water to retain the bright green color.
2. Lightly toast the sliced almonds in a dry skillet until golden brown.
3. Wash and dry the salad greens thoroughly.
4. In a small bowl, mix olive oil, apple cider vinegar, honey, Dijon mustard, salt, and pepper to prepare the dressing.
5. In a salad bowl, combine the broccoli, greens, dried cranberries, and toasted almonds. Drizzle with the dressing and gently toss.

Serve immediately to enjoy the fresh flavors and textures.

NUTRITION (PER 100 G): 120 kcal, 3 g protein, 6 g fat, 13 g carbs, 3 g fiber.

GARNISHING TIP: For decoration, add a few extra dried cranberries or sprinkle the salad with crushed almonds.

CITRUS FRESHNESS: SALAD WITH BABY SPINACH, GRAPEFRUIT, AND WALNUTS

DESCRIPTION: This salad brings together the tenderness of baby spinach, the juicy brightness of grapefruit, and the crunchy texture of toasted walnuts. A light citrus dressing with a subtle honey note enhances the freshness of the ingredients, making it a perfect choice for a spring lunch or light dinner filled with flavor and inspiration.

INGREDIENTS:

- 3 1/2 oz (100 g) baby spinach
- 1 large grapefruit (about 300 g)
- 1/4 cup (30 g) walnuts, lightly toasted
- 2 tbsp (30 ml) orange juice
- 1 tbsp (15 ml) lemon juice
- 1 tsp (5 ml) honey
- 1 tbsp (15 ml) olive oil
- Pinch of salt and freshly ground pepper

COOKING TIME: 10 minutes

INSTRUCTIONS:
1. Peel the grapefruit, removing the skin and white membrane. Cut the flesh into segments or pieces.
2. Wash and dry the baby spinach thoroughly.
3. Lightly toast the walnuts in a dry skillet until golden brown.
4. In a small bowl, mix orange juice, lemon juice, honey, olive oil, salt, and pepper to prepare the dressing.
5. In a salad bowl, combine the spinach, grapefruit, and walnuts. Drizzle with the dressing and gently toss.
6. Serve the salad immediately to enjoy its fresh and vibrant flavors.

NUTRITION (PER 100 G): 85 kcal, 2 g protein, 5 g fat, 8 g carbs, 2 g fiber.

GARNISHING TIP: Add a few extra grapefruit segments or sprinkle with chopped walnuts for a decorative touch.

NATURE'S INSPIRATION: SALAD WITH SPRING HERBS AND PINE NUTS

DESCRIPTION: This light salad combines the freshness of spring herbs with the refined nutty flavor of toasted pine nuts. A delicate lemon dressing enhances the natural aromas, creating a dish that is perfect for a spring lunch or dinner, filling your plate with simplicity and elegance.

INGREDIENTS:
- 3 1/2 oz (100 g) mix of spring herbs (dill, parsley, mint, cilantro)
- 1/4 cup (30 g) pine nuts, lightly toasted
- 2 tbsp (30 ml) olive oil
- 1 tbsp (15 ml) lemon juice
- 1 tsp (5 ml) honey
- Pinch of salt and freshly ground pepper

COOKING TIME: 10 minutes

INSTRUCTIONS:
1. Wash the spring herbs, pat them dry, and coarsely chop.
2. Lightly toast the pine nuts in a dry skillet until golden brown.
3. In a small bowl, whisk together olive oil, lemon juice, honey, salt, and pepper to prepare the dressing.
4. In a salad bowl, combine the herbs and pine nuts. Drizzle with the dressing and gently toss.
5. Serve the salad immediately to enjoy its fresh flavors and aromas.

NUTRITION (PER 100 G): 90 kcal, 2 g protein, 7 g fat, 4 g carbs, 2 g fiber.

GARNISHING TIP: Decorate the salad with fresh mint sprigs or add a touch of grated lemon zest for an enhanced aroma.

TENDER GREENS: SALAD WITH BABY ASPARAGUS, PEAS, AND MINT DRESSING

DESCRIPTION: This salad combines the crunch of tender asparagus, the sweetness of fresh peas, and the refreshing notes of a mint dressing. Light, nutritious, and full of spring freshness, it's a perfect choice for lunch or dinner, bringing brightness and ease to your day.

INGREDIENTS:
- 1/2 bunch (150 g) baby asparagus
- 1 cup (150 g) fresh or frozen peas
- 3 1/2 oz (100 g) mixed salad greens
- 2 tbsp (30 ml) olive oil
- 1 tbsp (15 ml) lemon juice
- 1 tsp (5 ml) honey
- 2 tbsp (30 ml) mint purée (or finely chopped fresh mint leaves)
- Pinch of salt and freshly ground pepper

COOKING TIME: Prep: 10 minutes, Cook: 3 minutes

INSTRUCTIONS:
1. Wash the asparagus, trim the tough ends, and cut it into 2–3 cm pieces. Blanch in salted boiling water for 2 minutes, then rinse with cold water and pat dry.
2. If using frozen peas, thaw them in hot water for 1–2 minutes, then rinse with cold water and pat dry.
3. Wash and dry the salad greens thoroughly.
4. In a small bowl, whisk together olive oil, lemon juice, honey, mint purée, salt, and pepper to prepare the dressing.
5. In a salad bowl, combine the asparagus, peas, and greens. Drizzle with the dressing and gently toss.
6. Serve immediately to enjoy the fresh spring flavors.

NUTRITION (PER 100 G): 75 kcal, 3 g protein, 4 g fat, 7 g carbs, 2 g fiber.

GARNISHING TIP: Add a few fresh mint leaves and lemon slices for added brightness and aroma.

SUMMER SALADS: FRESHNESS AND THE ABUNDANCE OF SUNNY FLAVORS

Summer is a season when nature reveals its full richness, offering us vibrant colors, intense aromas, and a bountiful harvest. Summer salads capture the magnificence of this time: crisp vegetables, juicy fruits and berries, fresh herbs, and light protein additions make them indispensable on your table. These dishes not only refresh but also energize, perfectly aligning with the warmth and freedom of summer days.

Summer salads offer endless opportunities for creativity: sweet strawberries paired with tender spinach and balsamic vinegar, or watermelon with salty feta and fresh mint—such combinations surprise with their flavors and delight the eye. The fusion of vegetables like crunchy cucumbers, ripe tomatoes, and fragrant peppers with fruits and berries creates the ideal balance of textures and freshness, perfect for a hot summer day.

Grilled salads are equally enticing: zucchini, bell peppers, and corn prepared over an open flame and dressed with olive oil and herbs fill the dish with warmth and a light smoky aroma of a summer evening. Protein additions like grilled chicken breast, tender fish, or tofu make the salads more nourishing while preserving their lightness and natural flavors.

Dressings play a crucial role. Summer dressings should be as light and refreshing as the season itself. Lemon juice, orange zest, honey, basil, and mint create the perfect harmony of flavors, enhancing the freshness of the ingredients and adding brightness. They are simple and natural, making the salads not only delicious but also healthy.

Summer salads are versatile: they are perfect for picnics, barbecues, family dinners, and festive gatherings. Garnish them with fresh berries, edible flowers, and leafy greens to turn each dish into a work of art that fills your table with the magic of summer vibes.

Welcome to the world of summer salads! Let every recipe inspire you to create light and flavorful dishes that bring warmth and joy to every bite. Discover the magic of summer and savor its flavors to the fullest!

SUMMER DELIGHT: SALAD WITH WATERMELON, FETA, AND MINT

DESCRIPTION: This salad combines the juicy sweetness of watermelon, the salty tang of feta, and the refreshing notes of mint. A light dressing enhances the harmony of flavors, making it the perfect choice for a summer lunch or a light snack, filling your day with brightness and freshness.

INGREDIENTS:
- 3 cups (450 g) watermelon cubes, seedless
- 3 1/2 oz (100 g) feta cheese
- 1/4 cup (30 g) fresh mint leaves
- 2 tbsp (30 ml) olive oil
- 1 tbsp (15 ml) lemon juice
- Pinch of freshly ground black pepper
- A few lime slices for garnish

COOKING TIME: 10 minutes

INSTRUCTIONS:
1. Cut the watermelon into large cubes.
2. Dice the feta into small cubes or crumble it.
3. Wash and dry the mint leaves.
4. In a small bowl, mix olive oil, lemon juice, and pepper to prepare the dressing.
5. In a salad bowl, combine the watermelon, feta, and mint. Drizzle with the dressing and gently toss.
6. Garnish the salad with lime slices before serving.

NUTRITION (PER 100 G): 70 kcal, 2 g protein, 4 g fat, 6 g carbs, 1 g fiber.

GARNISHING TIP: For added vibrancy, include a few thin slices of watermelon with the rind or sprinkle the salad with grated lime zest.

ITALIAN CLASSIC: CAPRESE WITH TOMATOES AND FRESH BASIL

DESCRIPTION: Caprese is a harmony of flavors: the sweetness of ripe tomatoes, the tender texture of fresh mozzarella, and the vibrant aroma of basil. A light dressing of olive oil and balsamic vinegar enhances the elegance of this classic Italian dish, making it a perfect choice for a summer lunch or dinner.

INGREDIENTS:
- 2 large tomatoes (about 300 g)
- 7 oz (200 g) fresh mozzarella
- 10–12 fresh basil leaves
- 2 tbsp (30 ml) olive oil
- 1 tbsp (15 ml) balsamic vinegar
- Pinch of salt and freshly ground black pepper

COOKING TIME: 10 minutes

INSTRUCTIONS:
1. Slice the tomatoes and mozzarella into 1 cm thick rounds.
2. Arrange the tomato and mozzarella slices alternately on a serving plate.
3. Place basil leaves between the layers.
4. Mix olive oil, balsamic vinegar, salt, and pepper to prepare the dressing.
5. Drizzle the salad with the dressing just before serving.
6. Garnish with a few drops of balsamic glaze for added aroma and presentation.

NUTRITION (PER 100 G): 120 kcal, 6 g protein, 8 g fat, 5 g carbs, 1 g fiber.

GARNISHING TIP: Use fresh basil sprigs and a sprinkle of grated lemon zest for a touch of contrast and sophistication.

GARDEN COOL: REFRESHING CUCUMBER SALAD WITH YOGURT AND DILL

DESCRIPTION: This light salad combines the refreshing crunch of cucumbers, the creamy smoothness of yogurt, and the aromatic freshness of dill. It's a perfect choice for a summer lunch or side dish that brings coolness and ease to a hot day.

INGREDIENTS:
- 2 large cucumbers (about 300 g)
- 1/2 cup (120 ml) plain yogurt
- 2 tbsp (30 ml) lemon juice
- 1 tbsp (15 ml) olive oil
- 1 garlic clove, minced
- 1/4 cup (15 g) fresh dill, finely chopped
- Pinch of salt and freshly ground black pepper

COOKING TIME: 10 minutes

INSTRUCTIONS:
1. Wash the cucumbers and slice them into thin rounds or half-moons.
2. In a small bowl, mix the yogurt, lemon juice, olive oil, garlic, dill, salt, and pepper to prepare the dressing.
3. In a salad bowl, combine the cucumbers with the dressing. Toss thoroughly to coat each slice evenly.
4. Serve the salad chilled to enhance its refreshing qualities.

NUTRITION (PER 100 G): 50 kcal, 2 g protein, 3 g fat, 4 g carbs, 1 g fiber.

GARNISHING TIP: Top with a sprig of fresh dill and a light sprinkle of ground black pepper for added visual appeal.

SUMMER ABUNDANCE: SALAD WITH CORN, AVOCADO, AND CHERRY TOMATOES

DESCRIPTION: This salad blends the sweetness of corn, the creamy tenderness of avocado, and the juiciness of cherry tomatoes. A light lime dressing with zesty accents highlights the natural flavors, making it a perfect choice for a summer lunch or dinner filled with freshness and vibrancy.

INGREDIENTS:
- 1 cup (150 g) cooked or canned corn
- 1 ripe avocado
- 1 cup (150 g) cherry tomatoes
- 3 1/2 oz (100 g) salad greens (arugula, spinach)
- 2 tbsp (30 ml) olive oil
- 1 tbsp (15 ml) lime juice
- Pinch of salt and freshly ground black pepper

COOKING TIME: 10 minutes

INSTRUCTIONS:
1. If using canned corn, drain it; if fresh, boil it until tender.
2. Cut the avocado into cubes.
3. Halve the cherry tomatoes.
4. Wash and dry the salad greens thoroughly.
5. In a small bowl, whisk together olive oil, lime juice, salt, and pepper to prepare the dressing.
6. In a salad bowl, combine the corn, avocado, cherry tomatoes, and greens. Drizzle with the dressing and gently toss.
7. Serve immediately to enjoy the freshness of the ingredients.

NUTRITION (PER 100 G): 85 kcal, 2 g protein, 6 g fat, 7 g carbs, 2 g fiber.

GARNISHING TIP: For a bright accent, garnish the salad with thin lime slices or add a few fresh cilantro leaves.

BERRY MAGIC: SALAD WITH BLUEBERRIES, RASPBERRIES, AND ARUGULA

DESCRIPTION: This salad combines the sweetness of fresh berries, the zesty freshness of arugula, and the lightness of a honey-lemon dressing. Bright flavors and contrasting textures create a harmonious dish, perfect for a summer snack or a light dinner.

INGREDIENTS:
- 3 1/2 oz (100 g) arugula
- 1/2 cup (75 g) fresh blueberries
- 1/2 cup (75 g) fresh raspberries
- 2 tbsp (30 g) sliced almonds, lightly toasted
- 2 tbsp (30 ml) olive oil
- 1 tbsp (15 ml) lemon juice
- 1 tsp (5 ml) honey
- Pinch of salt and freshly ground black pepper

COOKING TIME: 10 minutes

INSTRUCTIONS:
1. Wash and dry the arugula and berries thoroughly.
2. Lightly toast the sliced almonds in a dry skillet until golden brown.
3. In a small bowl, whisk together olive oil, lemon juice, honey, salt, and pepper to prepare the dressing.
4. In a salad bowl, combine the arugula, blueberries, raspberries, and toasted almonds. Drizzle with the dressing and gently toss.
5. Serve immediately to enjoy the freshness of the berries and greens.

NUTRITION (PER 100 G): 75 kcal, 2 g protein, 5 g fat, 6 g carbs, 2 g fiber.

GARNISHING TIP: Decorate the salad with a few whole raspberries and blueberries for a vibrant touch, and sprinkle with a bit of lemon zest for added brightness.

TROPICAL BREEZE: SALAD WITH MANGO AND CILANTRO

DESCRIPTION: This salad combines the juicy sweetness of mango, refreshing notes of cilantro, and the tangy zest of a light lime dressing. A perfect choice for a light lunch or dinner that transports you to the tropics and offers unforgettable freshness.

INGREDIENTS:
- 1 large ripe mango (about 200 g), diced
- 3 1/2 oz (100 g) mixed salad greens (arugula, spinach, or a mix)
- 1/4 cup (15 g) fresh cilantro, chopped
- 2 tbsp (30 ml) olive oil
- 1 tbsp (15 ml) lime juice
- 1 tsp (5 ml) honey
- Pinch of salt and freshly ground black pepper
- A few lime slices for garnish

COOKING TIME: 10 minutes

INSTRUCTIONS:
1. Dice the mango into cubes.
2. Wash and dry the salad greens thoroughly.
3. Chop the fresh cilantro.
4. In a small bowl, whisk together olive oil, lime juice, honey, salt, and pepper to prepare the dressing.
5. In a salad bowl, combine the greens, mango, and cilantro. Drizzle with the dressing and gently toss.
6. Garnish the salad with lime slices before serving.

NUTRITION (PER 100 G): 85 kcal, 1 g protein, 4 g fat, 11 g carbs, 2 g fiber.

GARNISHING TIP: Add a few whole cilantro leaves and a sprinkle of grated lime zest for an extra burst of freshness.

SWEET SUMMER EVENING: SALAD WITH PEACHES, MOZZARELLA, AND BASIL

DESCRIPTION: This sophisticated salad combines the sweetness of juicy peaches, the tender texture of mozzarella, and the vibrant aroma of fresh basil. A light honey-balsamic dressing adds harmony to the flavors, making it an ideal choice for a summer dinner or an elegant appetizer filled with freshness and charm.

INGREDIENTS:
- 2 ripe peaches (about 300 g)
- 7 oz (200 g) fresh mozzarella
- 10–12 fresh basil leaves
- 2 tbsp (30 ml) olive oil
- 1 tbsp (15 ml) balsamic vinegar
- 1 tsp (5 ml) honey
- Pinch of salt and freshly ground black pepper

COOKING TIME: 10 minutes

INSTRUCTIONS:
1. Slice the peaches into thin wedges.
2. Cut the mozzarella into slices or small cubes.
3. Wash and dry the basil leaves thoroughly.
4. In a small bowl, whisk together olive oil, balsamic vinegar, honey, salt, and pepper to prepare the dressing.
5. On a serving plate, arrange the peach slices, mozzarella, and basil leaves, alternating them. Drizzle with the dressing just before serving.
6. Garnish with a few drops of balsamic glaze for an extra flavor boost.

NUTRITION (PER 100 G): 100 kcal, 5 g protein, 6 g fat, 7 g carbs, 1 g fiber.

GARNISHING TIP: Add a sprig of basil and a touch of grated lemon zest for a bright, decorative accent.

MEDITERRANEAN LIGHTNESS: SUMMER SALAD WITH PASTA, OLIVES, AND CHERRY TOMATOES

DESCRIPTION: This salad combines the lightness of pasta, the juiciness of cherry tomatoes, and the tangy notes of olives. A simple dressing of olive oil and lemon juice infuses the dish with Mediterranean flavors, making it an ideal choice for a summer lunch or an outdoor picnic.

INGREDIENTS:
- 1 1/2 cups (150 g) cooked pasta (penne, fusilli, or farfalle)
- 1 cup (150 g) cherry tomatoes, halved
- 1/4 cup (50 g) black olives, halved
- 3 1/2 oz (100 g) salad greens (arugula, spinach, or a mix)
- 2 tbsp (30 ml) olive oil
- 1 tbsp (15 ml) lemon juice
- 1 garlic clove, minced
- Pinch of salt and freshly ground black pepper
- A few basil leaves for garnish

COOKING TIME: Prep: 10 minutes, Cook pasta: 10 minutes

INSTRUCTIONS:
1. Cook the pasta in salted water until al dente. Rinse with cold water and drain thoroughly.
2. Halve the cherry tomatoes and olives.
3. Wash and dry the salad greens thoroughly.
4. In a small bowl, whisk together olive oil, lemon juice, garlic, salt, and pepper to prepare the dressing.
5. In a large bowl, combine the pasta, cherry tomatoes, olives, and greens. Drizzle with the dressing and gently toss.
6. Serve the salad chilled, garnished with basil leaves.

NUTRITION (PER 100 G): 120 kcal, 3 g protein, 4 g fat, 16 g carbs, 2 g fiber.

GARNISHING TIP: Add a sprinkle of grated Parmesan or a drizzle of balsamic glaze for enhanced flavor and richness.

ASIAN HARMONY: SALAD WITH RED CABBAGE, CARROTS, AND SESAME DRESSING

DESCRIPTION: This vibrant salad combines the crunchy texture of red cabbage and carrots with the rich flavors of sesame dressing. Light, nutritious, and packed with taste accents, it is the perfect choice for a lunch or dinner with an Asian flair, adding sophistication and freshness to your table.

INGREDIENTS:
- 2 cups (150 g) thinly shredded red cabbage
- 1 large carrot (about 100 g), grated or julienned
- 1/4 cup (30 g) chopped green onions
- 2 tbsp (30 ml) sesame oil
- 1 tbsp (15 ml) soy sauce
- 1 tsp (5 ml) rice vinegar
- 1 tsp honey or maple syrup
- 1 tbsp (10 g) toasted sesame seeds

COOKING TIME: 10 minutes

INSTRUCTIONS:
1. Thinly shred the red cabbage into strips.
2. Peel the carrot and grate it on a large grater or slice it into thin matchsticks.
3. Finely chop the green onions.
4. In a small bowl, whisk together sesame oil, soy sauce, rice vinegar, and honey to prepare the dressing.
5. In a salad bowl, combine the cabbage, carrots, and green onions. Drizzle with the dressing and toss well.
6. Sprinkle the salad with toasted sesame seeds before serving.

NUTRITION (PER 100 G): 80 kcal, 2 g protein, 5 g fat, 7 g carbs, 2 g fiber.

GARNISHING TIP: For added aroma and flavor, garnish with fresh cilantro or thin slices of fresh chili.

SUMMER SPARK: SALAD WITH SHRIMP, PINEAPPLE, AND CHILI

DESCRIPTION: This vibrant and spicy salad combines the tender texture of shrimp, the sweetness of juicy pineapple, and the heat of fresh chili. A light lime dressing adds a tropical freshness, making it the perfect choice for a hot summer evening filled with exotic flavors.

INGREDIENTS:
- 7 oz (200 g) cooked and peeled shrimp
- 1 cup (150 g) fresh pineapple, diced
- 1/2 fresh red chili, thinly sliced
- 3 1/2 oz (100 g) salad greens (arugula, spinach, or a mix)
- 2 tbsp (30 ml) olive oil
- 1 tbsp (15 ml) lime juice
- Pinch of salt and freshly ground black pepper
- A few lime slices for garnish

COOKING TIME: 10 minutes

INSTRUCTIONS:
1. If using frozen shrimp, thaw them and pat dry with a paper towel.
2. Dice the pineapple into cubes.
3. Thinly slice the red chili into rings.
4. Wash and dry the salad greens thoroughly.
5. In a small bowl, whisk together olive oil, lime juice, salt, and pepper to prepare the dressing.
6. In a salad bowl, combine the greens, shrimp, pineapple, and chili. Drizzle with the dressing and gently toss.
7. Garnish with lime slices before serving.

NUTRITION (PER 100 G): 90 kcal, 10 g protein, 4 g fat, 5 g carbs, 1 g fiber.

GARNISHING TIP: Add a few fresh mint leaves for contrast or sprinkle with grated lime zest for extra aroma and flavor.

SUMMER GARDEN: SALAD WITH TOMATOES, CUCUMBERS, AND BELL PEPPERS

DESCRIPTION: This classic summer salad brings together crunchy vegetables, the juicy aroma of bell peppers, and the lightness of an olive oil-based dressing. A simple and refreshing dish, perfect for lunch or dinner on a hot day.

INGREDIENTS:
- 2 large tomatoes (about 300 g), diced
- 2 medium cucumbers (about 300 g), sliced into half-moons
- 1 large bell pepper (about 150 g), cut into thin strips
- 1/4 cup (15 g) fresh parsley, finely chopped
- 2 tbsp (30 ml) olive oil
- 1 tbsp (15 ml) lemon juice
- Pinch of salt and freshly ground black pepper

COOKING TIME: 10 minutes

INSTRUCTIONS:
1. Dice the tomatoes, slice the cucumbers into half-moons, and cut the bell pepper into thin strips.
2. Finely chop the parsley.
3. In a small bowl, whisk together olive oil, lemon juice, salt, and pepper to prepare the dressing.
4. In a salad bowl, combine the tomatoes, cucumbers, bell pepper, and parsley. Drizzle with the dressing and gently toss.
5. Serve immediately to preserve the freshness of the vegetables.

NUTRITION (PER 100 G): 45 kcal, 1 g protein, 3 g fat, 4 g carbs, 1 g fiber.

GARNISHING TIP: Decorate the salad with fresh parsley leaves or add a few thin rings of red onion for a pop of color and extra flavor.

FRUITY BLAST: SALAD WITH PINEAPPLE, KIWI, AND FRESH MINT

DESCRIPTION: This tropical salad combines the sweetness of pineapple, the tenderness of kiwi, and the freshness of mint. A light honey-lime dressing highlights the vibrant flavors, making it a perfect choice for a summer dessert or snack.

INGREDIENTS:
- 1 cup (150 g) fresh pineapple, diced
- 2 medium kiwis, sliced
- 1/4 cup (15 g) fresh mint, finely chopped
- 2 tbsp (30 ml) lime juice
- 1 tsp (5 ml) honey
- Pinch of freshly ground black pepper (optional)

COOKING TIME: 10 minutes

INSTRUCTIONS:
1. Dice the pineapple into cubes and slice the kiwi into thin rounds.
2. Finely chop the fresh mint leaves.
3. In a small bowl, mix lime juice and honey. If desired, add a pinch of black pepper for a spicy kick.
4. In a salad bowl, combine the pineapple, kiwi, and mint. Drizzle with the dressing and gently toss.
5. Serve immediately to enjoy the tropical freshness.

NUTRITION (PER 100 G): 60 kcal, 0.5 g protein, 1 g fat, 14 g carbs, 2 g fiber.

GARNISHING TIP: Decorate the salad with mint leaves or lime slices for a bright and appealing accent.

AUTUMN SYMPHONY: WARMTH AND FLAVOR OF THE GOLDEN SEASON

Autumn is a time of golden leaves, crisp air, and cozy evenings. It's the season when nature delights us with its richest colors and bountiful harvest. As the days grow cooler, we crave the warmth of home, deeper flavors, and the use of seasonal ingredients gifted by the fall harvest. This section is a celebration of autumn's magic—warm, hearty, rich, and harmonious dishes that will fill your home with comfort and warmth.

Autumn salads blend the vibrant colors and textures of the season, turning every dish into a feast of flavors. The stars of our autumn salads are pumpkin, sweet potatoes, beets, red cabbage, apples, and nuts. Pumpkin, with its sweet and tender texture, adds depth and richness. Beets bring earthy and robust notes, while apples contribute a refreshing sweet-tart crispness that balances and lightens the dishes.

This section also includes recipes featuring grains such as quinoa and bulgur, alongside roasted root vegetables. These ingredients not only make the salads nutritious but also add intriguing textures. For instance, a salad with roasted pumpkin, goat cheese, and nuts pairs beautifully with a honey-mustard dressing, creating a symphony of flavors where the sweetness of pumpkin mingles with the tanginess of cheese and the crunch of nuts. Such dishes not only nourish but also evoke comfort and joy with every bite.

Many of these autumn salads are enriched with protein-packed ingredients to provide the sustenance needed during colder months. Some recipes feature grilled chicken, shrimp, or mushrooms, which add aromatic and textural variety. Pan-fried mushrooms like button mushrooms or chanterelles are especially suited for fall dishes, bringing a forest-inspired touch and enhancing the depth of flavors.

These salads are perfect for both everyday meals and special occasions, adding a sense of coziness and warmth to your table. Garnish them with pomegranate seeds, fresh greens, or apple slices to add brightness and create a festive mood. Fragrant herbs like thyme and rosemary make an excellent addition, enhancing the natural flavors and evoking a sense of connection with the earth.

Dressings play a pivotal role in crafting the flavors of autumn salads. This section features recipes for warm dressings that highlight the softness and richness of the ingredients. Honey-mustard dressing or a blend of balsamic vinegar and olive oil adds harmony to the salads, making them even more flavorful and exciting. These dressings reveal the subtle nuances of each ingredient, transforming a simple salad into a culinary masterpiece.

Welcome to the world of autumn salads—may these recipes fill your home with the aromas of fall, bring warmth, and create a cozy atmosphere. Immerse yourself in this symphony of flavors and savor every moment when nature and the kitchen unite to bring you joy and inspiration.

AUTUMN HARMONY: WARM SALAD WITH PUMPKIN, BEETS, AND GOAT CHEESE

DESCRIPTION: This cozy autumn salad combines the sweetness of roasted pumpkin and beets with the creaminess of goat cheese. A light dressing of olive oil and balsamic vinegar enhances the depth of flavor, making it a perfect choice for lunch or dinner.

INGREDIENTS:
- 2 cups (300 g) pumpkin, cubed
- 2 medium beets (about 300 g), peeled and sliced
- 3 1/2 oz (100 g) salad greens (arugula, spinach, or a mix)
- 2 oz (60 g) goat cheese, sliced or crumbled
- 2 tbsp (30 ml) olive oil (for roasting)
- 1 tbsp (15 ml) balsamic vinegar
- 1 tbsp (15 ml) olive oil (for dressing)
- Pinch of salt and freshly ground black pepper
- A few walnuts (optional)

COOKING TIME: Prep: 15 minutes, Cook: 25 minutes

INSTRUCTIONS:
1. Preheat the oven to 200°C (390°F).
2. Cube the pumpkin and slice the beets. Place the vegetables on a baking tray, drizzle with 2 tbsp olive oil, season with salt and pepper, and roast for 20–25 minutes until tender and slightly golden.
3. Wash and dry the salad greens.
4. In a small bowl, mix 1 tbsp olive oil with balsamic vinegar to prepare the dressing.
5. In a salad bowl, combine the roasted vegetables, salad greens, and goat cheese. Drizzle with the dressing and gently toss to combine.
6. Serve warm, adding walnuts for extra texture if desired.

NUTRITION (PER 100 G): 120 kcal, 3 g protein, 6 g fat, 12 g carbs, 3 g fiber.

GARNISHING TIP: Decorate the salad with sprigs of fresh thyme or add a few drops of balsamic glaze for a richer flavor profile.

VELVET EVENING: COUSCOUS SALAD WITH POMEGRANATE AND PINE NUTS

DESCRIPTION: This salad combines the lightness of couscous, the sweetness of pomegranate seeds, and the nutty flavor of toasted pine nuts. A light citrus dressing enhances the harmony of flavors, making it a perfect choice for a cozy dinner.

INGREDIENTS:
- 1 cup (150 g) cooked couscous
- 1/2 cup (75 g) pomegranate seeds
- 1/4 cup (30 g) pine nuts, lightly toasted
- 3 1/2 oz (100 g) salad greens (arugula, spinach, or a mix)
- 2 tbsp (30 ml) orange juice
- 1 tbsp (15 ml) lemon juice
- 1 tbsp (15 ml) olive oil
- Pinch of salt and freshly ground black pepper
- A few fresh mint leaves (optional)

COOKING TIME: Prep: 10 minutes, Cooking: 5 minutes

INSTRUCTIONS:
1. Cook the couscous according to the package instructions and let it cool.
2. Lightly toast the pine nuts in a dry skillet until golden brown.
3. Wash and dry the salad greens.
4. In a small bowl, whisk together orange juice, lemon juice, olive oil, salt, and pepper to prepare the dressing.
5. In a salad bowl, combine the couscous, pomegranate seeds, greens, and pine nuts. Drizzle with the dressing and gently toss to mix.
6. Optionally, garnish the salad with fresh mint leaves before serving.

NUTRITION (PER 100 G): 95 kcal, 2 g protein, 4 g fat, 12 g carbs, 2 g fiber.

GARNISHING TIP: Add a few extra pomegranate seeds and a sprinkle of freshly grated orange zest for a vibrant finish.

SWEET AUTUMN: ROASTED CARROT SALAD WITH HONEY AND PECANS

DESCRIPTION: This salad combines the caramelized sweetness of roasted carrots, the crunch of pecans, and the rich aroma of honey. It's a perfect choice for a cozy autumn lunch or dinner, bringing warmth and seasonal flavors to your table.
INGREDIENTS:
- 4 medium carrots (about 400 g), cut into sticks
- 2 tbsp (30 ml) olive oil
- 1 tbsp (15 ml) honey
- 1/4 cup (30 g) pecans, lightly toasted
- 3 1/2 oz (100 g) salad greens (arugula, spinach, or mix)
- 1 tbsp (15 ml) apple cider vinegar
- 1 tsp (5 ml) Dijon mustard
- Pinch of salt and freshly ground black pepper

COOKING TIME: Prep: 10 minutes, Cooking: 20 minutes
INSTRUCTIONS:
1. Preheat the oven to 200°C (390°F).
2. Cut the carrots into sticks, place them on a baking sheet, drizzle with 1 tbsp of olive oil, season with salt and pepper. Roast for 15–20 minutes until tender and lightly caramelized.
3. Lightly toast the pecans in a dry skillet until fragrant.
4. In a small bowl, mix honey, apple cider vinegar, Dijon mustard, and the remaining olive oil to make the dressing.
5. Wash and dry the salad greens.
6. In a salad bowl, combine the roasted carrots, greens, and pecans. Drizzle with the dressing and gently toss.
7. Serve warm and enjoy the cozy autumn flavors.

NUTRITION (PER 100 G): 110 kcal, 2 g protein, 7 g fat, 9 g carbs, 2 g fiber.
GARNISHING TIP: For a burst of brightness, add some grated orange zest or decorate with sprigs of fresh thyme.

AUTUMN DELIGHT: APPLE SALAD WITH WALNUTS AND MAPLE SYRUP

DESCRIPTION: This salad combines the crisp sweetness of apples, the crunch of toasted walnuts, and the rich flavor of maple syrup. It's a perfect choice for an autumn snack or light dinner, bringing the essence of the season to your plate.
INGREDIENTS:
- 2 medium apples (about 300 g), thinly sliced
- 1/4 cup (30 g) walnuts, lightly toasted
- 3 1/2 oz (100 g) salad greens (arugula, spinach, or mix)
- 2 tbsp (30 ml) olive oil
- 1 tbsp (15 ml) maple syrup
- 1 tbsp (15 ml) apple cider vinegar
- Pinch of salt and freshly ground black pepper
- A few sprigs of fresh thyme for garnish (optional)

COOKING TIME: Prep: 10 minutes
INSTRUCTIONS:
1. Thinly slice the apples.
2. Lightly toast the walnuts in a dry skillet until golden and fragrant.
3. Wash and dry the salad greens.
4. In a small bowl, mix olive oil, maple syrup, apple cider vinegar, salt, and pepper to prepare the dressing.
5. In a salad bowl, combine the greens, apple slices, and toasted walnuts. Drizzle with the dressing and gently toss.
6. Garnish with thyme sprigs, if desired, before serving.

NUTRITION (PER 100 G): 90 kcal, 2 g protein, 6 g fat, 8 g carbs, 2 g fiber.
GARNISHING TIP: For added flavor, sprinkle grated lemon zest or drizzle a bit of extra maple syrup over the salad before serving.

CRUNCHY COMFORT: CABBAGE SALAD WITH TOASTED SEEDS

DESCRIPTION: This light and nutritious salad pairs the crispness of shredded cabbage with the crunch of toasted seeds. A simple lemon dressing highlights the natural flavors, making this dish perfect for lunch or dinner.

INGREDIENTS:
- 2 cups (150 g) finely shredded white or Savoy cabbage
- 1/4 cup (30 g) sunflower or pumpkin seeds, lightly toasted
- 3 1/2 oz (100 g) salad greens (arugula, spinach, or mix)
- 2 tbsp (30 ml) olive oil
- 1 tbsp (15 ml) lemon juice
- Pinch of salt and freshly ground black pepper

COOKING TIME: Prep: 10 minutes

INSTRUCTIONS:
1. Shred the cabbage into thin strips and gently massage it with your hands to soften.
2. Lightly toast the seeds in a dry skillet until golden and fragrant.
3. Wash and dry the salad greens.
4. In a small bowl, whisk together olive oil, lemon juice, salt, and pepper to prepare the dressing.
5. In a salad bowl, combine the cabbage, greens, and toasted seeds. Drizzle with the dressing and toss gently to combine.
6. Serve immediately to enjoy the salad's crisp texture and fresh flavor.

NUTRITION (PER 100 G): 65 kcal, 2 g protein, 4 g fat, 5 g carbs, 2 g fiber.

GARNISHING TIP: Sprinkle a few whole seeds on top and add a touch of grated lemon zest for a bright and decorative finish.

AUTUMN FLAME: ROASTED BRUSSELS SPROUT AND BACON SALAD

DESCRIPTION: This hearty salad combines golden, roasted Brussels sprouts, crispy bacon, and a tangy balsamic dressing. Its warm, rich flavors make it the perfect choice for a cozy autumn dinner.

INGREDIENTS:
- 2 cups (300 g) Brussels sprouts, halved
- 4 slices (50 g) bacon, chopped
- 3 1/2 oz (100 g) salad greens (arugula, spinach, or mix)
- 2 tbsp (30 ml) olive oil
- 1 tbsp (15 ml) balsamic vinegar
- 1 tsp (5 ml) honey
- Pinch of salt and freshly ground black pepper

COOKING TIME: Prep: 10 minutes, Cook: 15 minutes

INSTRUCTIONS:
1. Heat a skillet over medium heat. Fry the bacon pieces until crispy. Transfer to a paper towel to drain excess grease.
2. In the same skillet, using the remaining bacon fat, roast the Brussels sprouts cut-side down until golden and caramelized (about 7–10 minutes). Add a little olive oil if needed.
3. Wash and dry the salad greens.
4. In a small bowl, whisk together olive oil, balsamic vinegar, honey, salt, and pepper to prepare the dressing.
5. In a salad bowl, combine the salad greens, roasted Brussels sprouts, and bacon. Drizzle with the dressing and toss gently to mix.
6. Serve warm, enjoying the rich and comforting flavors of fall.

NUTRITION (PER 100 G): 150 kcal, 6 g protein, 10 g fat, 8 g carbs, 3 g fiber.

GARNISHING TIP: Drizzle a few drops of balsamic glaze and sprinkle thinly sliced green onions on top for an added touch of flavor and elegance.

PUMPKIN INSPIRATION: ROASTED PUMPKIN AND QUINOA SALAD

DESCRIPTION: This nourishing salad combines the caramelized sweetness of roasted pumpkin, the lightness of quinoa, and the aroma of fresh thyme. A simple olive oil and lemon dressing highlights the natural flavors, making this dish perfect for an autumn lunch or dinner.

INGREDIENTS:
- 2 cups (300 g) cubed pumpkin
- 1/2 cup (100 g) cooked quinoa
- 3 1/2 oz (100 g) salad greens (arugula, spinach, or mix)
- 1 tbsp (15 ml) olive oil (for roasting)
- 2 tbsp (30 ml) olive oil (for dressing)
- 1 tbsp (15 ml) lemon juice
- Pinch of salt and freshly ground black pepper
- A few sprigs of fresh thyme (optional)

COOKING TIME: Prep: 10 minutes, Cooking: 25 minutes

INSTRUCTIONS:
1. Preheat the oven to 200°C (390°F).
2. Cut the pumpkin into cubes and place them on a baking sheet. Drizzle with 1 tablespoon of olive oil, season with salt and pepper, and roast for 20–25 minutes until tender and slightly caramelized.
3. Cook the quinoa according to the package instructions and let it cool.
4. Wash and dry the salad greens.
5. In a small bowl, mix 2 tablespoons of olive oil, lemon juice, salt, and pepper to prepare the dressing.
6. In a salad bowl, combine the salad greens, roasted pumpkin, and quinoa. Drizzle with the dressing and gently toss.
7. Garnish with fresh thyme before serving, if desired.

NUTRITION (PER 100 G): 110 kcal, 3 g protein, 6 g fat, 10 g carbs, 2 g fiber.

GARNISHING TIP: Add a pop of color and sweetness by sprinkling a few pomegranate seeds or grating some orange zest on top.

FOREST FLAVOR: SAUTÉED MUSHROOM AND ARUGULA SALAD

DESCRIPTION: This warm and hearty salad combines the earthy aroma of sautéed mushrooms with the peppery bite of arugula and a light lemon dressing. It's a comforting dish perfect for a cozy lunch or dinner.

INGREDIENTS:
- 2 cups (200 g) fresh mushrooms (button, oyster, or wild mushrooms), sliced
- 3 1/2 oz (100 g) arugula
- 2 tbsp (30 ml) olive oil
- 1 tbsp (15 ml) lemon juice
- 1 garlic clove, finely chopped
- Pinch of salt and freshly ground black pepper
- 1 tbsp (10 g) toasted pine nuts (optional)

COOKING TIME: Prep: 10 minutes, Cooking: 10 minutes

INSTRUCTIONS:
1. Heat a skillet over medium heat. Add 1 tablespoon of olive oil and the garlic, sautéing until fragrant (about 30 seconds).
2. Add the mushrooms and cook for 7–10 minutes until golden and tender. Season with salt and pepper.
3. Wash and dry the arugula.
4. In a small bowl, mix the remaining tablespoon of olive oil, lemon juice, salt, and pepper to make the dressing.
5. In a salad bowl, combine the arugula and sautéed mushrooms. Drizzle with the dressing and toss gently.
6. Optionally, garnish with toasted pine nuts for added crunch.

NUTRITION (PER 100 G): 90 kcal, 3 g protein, 6 g fat, 6 g carbs, 2 g fiber.

GARNISHING TIP: Sprinkle with grated Parmesan or fresh thyme leaves for an extra layer of flavor.

ELEGANT AUTUMN: PEAR, WALNUT, AND BLUE CHEESE SALAD

DESCRIPTION: This sophisticated salad blends the sweetness of juicy pears, the crunch of toasted walnuts, and the bold flavor of blue cheese. A light honey mustard dressing perfectly ties the dish together, making it ideal for an autumn dinner or special occasion.

INGREDIENTS:
- 2 ripe pears (approx. 300 g), thinly sliced
- 1/4 cup (30 g) toasted walnuts
- 2 oz (60 g) crumbled blue cheese
- 3 1/2 oz (100 g) salad greens (arugula, spinach, or mix)
- 2 tbsp (30 ml) olive oil
- 1 tbsp (15 ml) apple cider vinegar
- 1 tsp (5 ml) honey
- 1 tsp (5 ml) Dijon mustard
- Pinch of salt and freshly ground black pepper

COOKING TIME: Prep: 10 minutes

INSTRUCTIONS:
1. Slice the pears thinly.
2. Lightly toast the walnuts in a dry skillet until golden.
3. Wash and dry the salad greens.
4. In a small bowl, whisk together olive oil, apple cider vinegar, honey, mustard, salt, and pepper to make the dressing.
5. In a salad bowl, combine the greens, pear slices, walnuts, and blue cheese. Drizzle with the dressing and toss gently.
6. Serve immediately, enjoying the rich autumnal flavors.

NUTRITION (PER 100 G): 110 kcal, 3 g protein, 7 g fat, 8 g carbs, 2 g fiber.

GARNISHING TIP: Drizzle with a touch of honey and garnish with a few whole walnuts for added visual appeal.

ROOT POWER: SALAD WITH ROOT VEGETABLES AND VINAIGRETTE

DESCRIPTION: This hearty salad combines vibrant root vegetables, rich flavors, and the lightness of a classic vinaigrette dressing. A perfect choice for an autumn lunch or dinner to savor nature's bounty.

INGREDIENTS:
- 1 medium beet (approx. 200 g), roasted and diced
- 1 large carrot (approx. 150 g), grated
- 1/2 medium celery root (approx. 150 g), grated
- 1/4 cup (30 g) toasted pumpkin or sunflower seeds
- 3 1/2 oz (100 g) salad greens (arugula, spinach, or mix)
- 2 tbsp (30 ml) olive oil
- 1 tbsp (15 ml) apple cider vinegar
- 1 tsp (5 ml) Dijon mustard
- 1 tsp (5 ml) honey
- Pinch of salt and freshly ground black pepper

COOKING TIME: Prep: 10 minutes, Cooking: 20 minutes

INSTRUCTIONS:
1. Roast the beet in the oven at 200°C (390°F) for 40–50 minutes until tender. Let cool, peel, and dice into cubes.
2. Place the grated carrot and celery root in a large salad bowl.
3. Lightly toast the pumpkin seeds in a dry skillet until golden.
4. Wash and dry the salad greens.
5. In a small bowl, whisk together olive oil, apple cider vinegar, Dijon mustard, honey, salt, and pepper to make the vinaigrette.
6. In the salad bowl, combine the beet, carrot, celery root, and salad greens. Drizzle with the vinaigrette and toss gently.
7. Sprinkle the salad with toasted seeds before serving.

NUTRITION (PER 100 G): 90 kcal, 2 g protein, 6 g fat, 8 g carbs, 2 g fiber.

GARNISHING TIP: Decorate the salad with a few sprigs of fresh thyme or pomegranate seeds for a pop of color and contrast.

WARM DELIGHT: LENTIL, SPINACH, AND ROASTED VEGETABLE SALAD

DESCRIPTION: This hearty and nourishing salad combines tender lentils, fresh spinach, and the rich flavors of roasted vegetables. A light mustard dressing enhances the natural tastes, making it a perfect choice for a cozy autumn or winter dinner.

INGREDIENTS:

- 1 cup (150 g) cooked green or brown lentils
- 1 small sweet potato (approx. 200 g), diced
- 1 red bell pepper (approx. 150 g), sliced
- 3 1/2 oz (100 g) fresh spinach
- 2 tbsp (30 ml) olive oil (for roasting)
- 1 tbsp (15 ml) olive oil (for dressing)
- 1 tbsp (15 ml) apple cider vinegar
- 1 tsp (5 ml) Dijon mustard
- Pinch of salt and freshly ground black pepper
- A few fresh parsley leaves (optional)

COOKING TIME: Prep: 10 minutes, Cooking: 25 minutes

INSTRUCTIONS:

1. Preheat the oven to 200°C (390°F).
2. Dice the sweet potato and slice the red bell pepper. Place them on a baking sheet, drizzle with 2 tbsp olive oil, and season with salt and pepper. Roast for 20–25 minutes until soft and slightly caramelized.
3. Wash and dry the spinach.
4. In a small bowl, whisk together 1 tbsp olive oil, apple cider vinegar, Dijon mustard, salt, and pepper for the dressing.
5. In a large salad bowl, combine the cooked lentils, roasted vegetables, and spinach. Drizzle with the dressing and toss gently.
6. Garnish with fresh parsley leaves before serving (optional).

NUTRITION (PER 100 G): 120 kcal, 4 g protein, 6 g fat, 13 g carbs, 3 g fiber.

GARNISHING TIP: Add a few drops of balsamic glaze or a sprinkle of grated lemon zest for an extra burst of flavor.

HARVEST INSPIRATION: WARM SALAD WITH SAUTÉED APPLES, SPINACH, AND PECANS

DESCRIPTION: This warm salad blends caramelized sautéed apples, tender spinach, and crunchy pecans. A light honey-mustard dressing enriches the flavors, making it a perfect choice for a cozy autumn lunch or dinner.

INGREDIENTS:

- 2 medium apples (approx. 300 g), thinly sliced
- 3 1/2 oz (100 g) fresh spinach
- 1/4 cup (30 g) pecans, lightly toasted
- 1 tbsp (15 ml) butter
- 1 tbsp (15 ml) honey (for apples)
- 1 tbsp (15 ml) olive oil (for dressing)
- 1 tbsp (15 ml) apple cider vinegar
- 1 tsp (5 ml) Dijon mustard
- Pinch of salt and freshly ground black pepper

COOKING TIME: Prep: 10 minutes, Cooking: 10 minutes

INSTRUCTIONS:

1. In a skillet, melt the butter over medium heat. Add the apple slices and honey. Sauté for 5–7 minutes until the apples are soft and lightly caramelized.
2. Toast the pecans in a dry skillet over medium heat until golden and fragrant.
3. Wash and dry the spinach.
4. In a small bowl, whisk together the olive oil, apple cider vinegar, Dijon mustard, salt, and pepper to prepare the dressing.
5. In a salad bowl, combine the spinach, sautéed apples, and pecans. Drizzle with the dressing and toss gently.
6. Serve the salad warm, enjoying its rich autumnal flavors.

NUTRITION (PER 100 G): 130 kcal, 2 g protein, 8 g fat, 13 g carbs, 2 g fiber.

GARNISHING TIP: Add a few thin slices of fresh apple or drizzle a little extra honey over the top for an elegant touch.

WINTER SALADS: WARMTH AND WINTER'S STRENGTH

Winter is a season that calls for warmth and coziness—a time when cold days inspire us to take extra care of our bodies and spirits. Winter salads are a blend of vibrant citrus notes, crunchy vegetables, and warming spices that add depth and richness to each dish. This section features recipes that warm the soul and energize the body, helping us embrace the winter chill with vitality.

Key Ingredients for Winter Wellness

Winter salads focus on ingredients rich in vitamins and minerals to boost immunity and resilience. Citrus fruits, pomegranates, root vegetables, and warming spices take center stage, creating unique and colorful dishes. Citrus fruits provide a refreshing tang and replenish much-needed vitamin C, while beets, carrots, and potatoes deliver essential nutrients to support the body during colder months.

A Balance of Light and Hearty

These salads offer a variety of options—from light and fresh dishes perfect for a simple dinner to heartier, warm salads ideal for cozy family gatherings. The inclusion of pomegranates, cranberries, and spiced dressings brings a touch of winter magic, transforming an ordinary meal into a true celebration.

Let these recipes be your allies in crafting a warm and inviting atmosphere at home. They'll fill your table with the essence of the season and your hearts with joy, no matter how cold it gets outside.

WINTER FRESHNESS — SALAD WITH CITRUS AND POMEGRANATE

DESCRIPTION: This vibrant winter salad combines juicy citrus fruits, crunchy pomegranate seeds, and a refreshing hint of mint. Simple and elegant, it's perfect as a light side or a festive dish.

INGREDIENTS:
- 2 oranges, peeled and sliced into rounds
- 1 grapefruit, peeled and segmented
- 1/2 cup (75 g) pomegranate seeds
- 3 1/2 ounces (100 g) salad greens (arugula or mix)
- 2 tablespoons (30 ml) olive oil
- 1 tablespoon (15 ml) lemon juice
- 1 teaspoon (5 ml) honey
- A few fresh mint leaves

COOKING TIME: Preparation: 10 minutes

INSTRUCTION:
1. Peel the oranges and grapefruit, remove the white pith, and cut into segments or slices.
2. Rinse the salad greens and pat them dry.
3. In a small bowl, whisk together olive oil, lemon juice, and honey for the dressing.
4. In a salad bowl, combine the greens, citrus fruits, and pomegranate seeds. Drizzle with the dressing and gently toss.
5. Garnish with fresh mint leaves before serving.

NUTRITIONAL VALUE (PER 100 G): 80 kcal, 1 g protein, 4 g fat, 11 g carbohydrates, 2 g fiber.

GARNISHING TIP: Add a sprinkle of grated orange zest to enhance the aroma and visual appeal.

WINTER WARMTH — ROASTED ROOT VEGETABLE SALAD WITH SPICES

DESCRIPTION: This hearty winter salad combines the sweetness of roasted root vegetables with the warm aromas of spices like cinnamon and cumin. Its cozy flavor makes it perfect for chilly winter days.

INGREDIENTS:
- 1 large carrot (approx. 150 g), cut into sticks
- 1 medium beet (approx. 200 g), diced
- 1/2 medium celery root (approx. 150 g), diced
- 2 tablespoons (30 ml) olive oil
- 1 teaspoon (5 g) ground cumin
- 1/2 teaspoon (2.5 g) cinnamon
- A pinch of salt and freshly ground black pepper
- 3 1/2 ounces (100 g) salad greens (arugula, spinach, or mix)
- 2 tablespoons (30 ml) orange juice
- 1 teaspoon (5 ml) honey
- 1 tablespoon (10 g) toasted pumpkin or sunflower seeds

COOKING TIME: Prep: 10 minutes, Cooking: 30 minutes

INSTRUCTIONS:
1. Preheat the oven to 200°C (390°F).
2. Cut the carrot, beet, and celery root. Place them in a bowl, add olive oil, cumin, cinnamon, salt, and pepper. Mix well.
3. Spread the root vegetables on a baking sheet and roast for 25–30 minutes, turning occasionally, until they are tender and slightly golden.
4. Rinse and pat dry the salad greens.
5. In a small bowl, combine orange juice and honey for the dressing.
6. In a salad bowl, mix the roasted vegetables and greens. Drizzle with the dressing and toss gently.
7. Sprinkle the salad with toasted seeds before serving.

NUTRITIONAL VALUE (PER 100 G): 120 kcal, 2 g protein, 6 g fat, 14 g carbs, 3 g fiber.

GARNISHING TIP: Add thin slices of fresh orange or a few pomegranate seeds for a vibrant touch.

WINTER CRUNCH — CABBAGE AND CARROT SALAD WITH SESAME DRESSING

DESCRIPTION: This fresh and crunchy salad combines thinly sliced cabbage, sweet carrots, and a nutty sesame dressing. A perfect choice for a winter lunch or dinner to add a splash of brightness to chilly days.

INGREDIENTS:
- 2 cups (150 g) thinly sliced white cabbage
- 1 large carrot (approx. 100 g), grated
- 1/4 cup (30 g) toasted sesame seeds
- 2 tablespoons (30 ml) sesame oil
- 1 tablespoon (15 ml) soy sauce
- 1 tablespoon (15 ml) rice vinegar
- 1 teaspoon (5 ml) honey
- A pinch of salt and freshly ground black pepper
- A few fresh cilantro leaves (optional)

COOKING TIME: Prep: 10 minutes

INSTRUCTIONS:
1. Thinly slice the cabbage and gently massage it with your hands to soften.
2. Peel and grate the carrot on a coarse grater.
3. Lightly toast sesame seeds in a dry skillet until golden.
4. In a small bowl, combine sesame oil, soy sauce, rice vinegar, honey, salt, and pepper to make the dressing.
5. In a salad bowl, combine cabbage, carrot, and sesame seeds. Drizzle with the dressing and mix gently.
6. Garnish the salad with cilantro leaves before serving (optional).

NUTRITIONAL VALUE (PER 100 G): 80 kcal, 2 g protein, 5 g fat, 7 g carbs, 2 g fiber.

GARNISHING TIP: Add a touch of finely sliced green onion or radish slices for extra color and texture.

CITRUS DELIGHT — SALAD WITH ORANGE, FENNEL, AND WALNUTS

DESCRIPTION: This refreshing salad combines the sweetness of oranges, the crunch of fennel, and the nutty taste of walnuts. A light honey-lemon dressing enhances the vibrant flavors, making this dish a perfect addition to your winter table.

INGREDIENTS:
- 2 large oranges, peeled and sliced into rounds
- 1 small fennel bulb (approx. 150 g), thinly sliced
- 1/4 cup (30 g) toasted walnuts
- 3 1/2 ounces (100 g) mixed salad greens (arugula, spinach, or a mix)
- 2 tablespoons (30 ml) olive oil
- 1 tablespoon (15 ml) lemon juice
- 1 teaspoon (5 ml) honey
- A pinch of salt and freshly ground black pepper
- A few fresh mint leaves (optional)

COOKING TIME: Prep: 10 minutes

INSTRUCTIONS:
1. Peel the oranges, remove the white pith, and slice them into rounds.
2. Thinly slice the fennel bulb. For a milder flavor, soak it in cold water for 5 minutes, then drain.
3. Lightly toast the walnuts in a dry skillet until golden.
4. Wash and dry the salad greens.
5. In a small bowl, whisk together olive oil, lemon juice, honey, salt, and pepper to make the dressing.
6. In a salad bowl, combine the salad greens, fennel, oranges, and walnuts. Drizzle with the dressing and toss gently.
7. Garnish with fresh mint leaves before serving (optional).

NUTRITIONAL VALUE (PER 100 G): 85 kcal, 2 g protein, 5 g fat, 9 g carbs, 2 g fiber.

GARNISHING TIP: Add some freshly grated orange zest to enhance the aroma and brighten the dish.

FESTIVE CHEER — SALAD WITH CRANBERRIES, SPINACH, AND FETA CHEESE

DESCRIPTION: This festive salad combines the rich flavors of juicy cranberries, tender spinach, and salty feta cheese. A light honey-balsamic dressing makes it perfect for a holiday table or a cozy winter dinner.
INGREDIENTS:
- 3 1/2 ounces (100 g) fresh spinach
- 1/4 cup (30 g) dried cranberries
- 2 ounces (60 g) crumbled feta cheese
- 1/4 cup (30 g) toasted walnuts
- 2 tablespoons (30 ml) olive oil
- 1 tablespoon (15 ml) balsamic vinegar
- 1 teaspoon (5 ml) honey
- A pinch of salt and freshly ground black pepper

COOKING TIME: Prep: 10 minutes
INSTRUCTIONS:
1. Wash and dry the spinach thoroughly.
2. Lightly toast the walnuts in a dry skillet until golden.
3. In a small bowl, whisk together olive oil, balsamic vinegar, honey, salt, and pepper to make the dressing.
4. In a salad bowl, combine the spinach, dried cranberries, crumbled feta cheese, and toasted walnuts. Drizzle with the dressing and toss gently.
5. Serve immediately and enjoy the festive flavors.

NUTRITIONAL VALUE (PER 100 G): 110 kcal, 3 g protein, 7 g fat, 8 g carbs, 2 g fiber.
GARNISHING TIP: Add a few extra cranberries and drizzle with balsamic glaze for a bright and contrasting touch.

WARM COMFORT — SALAD WITH POTATOES, GARLIC, AND ROSEMARY

DESCRIPTION: This warm salad combines fragrant roasted potatoes, garlic, and fresh rosemary. Simple yet rich in flavor, it's perfect for a winter lunch or dinner.
INGREDIENTS:
- 2 medium potatoes (about 300 g), cut into large chunks
- 2 garlic cloves, crushed
- 2 tablespoons (30 ml) olive oil
- 1 teaspoon (5 ml) lemon juice
- 1 sprig of fresh rosemary, finely chopped
- A pinch of salt and freshly ground black pepper
- 3 1/2 ounces (100 g) salad greens (arugula, spinach, or a mix)

COOKING TIME: Prep: 10 minutes, Cook: 30 minutes
INSTRUCTIONS:
1. Preheat the oven to 200°C (390°F).
2. Place the potato chunks on a baking sheet, drizzle with 1 tablespoon of olive oil, add the crushed garlic, rosemary, salt, and pepper. Toss to coat evenly.
3. Roast the potatoes for 25–30 minutes, turning occasionally, until golden and crispy.
4. Wash and dry the salad greens.
5. In a small bowl, whisk together the remaining tablespoon of olive oil and the lemon juice to make the dressing.
6. In a salad bowl, combine the salad greens with the roasted potatoes. Drizzle with the dressing and toss gently.
7. Serve the salad warm and enjoy its rich taste and aroma.

NUTRITIONAL VALUE (PER 100 G): 120 kcal, 2 g protein, 6 g fat, 14 g carbs, 2 g fiber.
GARNISHING TIP: Add a few sprigs of rosemary or a sprinkle of grated Parmesan for an enhanced aroma.

WINTER VIOLET — SALAD WITH RED CABBAGE AND APPLE CIDER VINEGAR

DESCRIPTION: This vibrant and refreshing salad combines the crunch of red cabbage with the gentle tang of apple cider vinegar. Light and nutritious, it's an excellent addition to a winter lunch or dinner.

INGREDIENTS:
- 2 cups (150 g) thinly shredded red cabbage
- 1 small carrot (about 100 g), grated
- 1/4 cup (30 g) toasted sunflower seeds
- 2 tablespoons (30 ml) apple cider vinegar
- 1 tablespoon (15 ml) olive oil
- 1 teaspoon (5 ml) honey
- A pinch of salt and freshly ground black pepper
- A few sprigs of fresh parsley for garnish (optional)

COOKING TIME: Prep: 10 minutes

INSTRUCTIONS:
1. Thinly shred the red cabbage and grate the carrot. Place them in a large bowl.
2. Lightly toast the sunflower seeds in a dry skillet until golden.
3. In a small bowl, whisk together apple cider vinegar, olive oil, honey, salt, and pepper to make the dressing.
4. Drizzle the dressing over the cabbage and carrot, mixing well to coat the vegetables evenly.
5. Sprinkle the salad with toasted sunflower seeds before serving.
6. Optionally, garnish with parsley leaves for added brightness.

NUTRITIONAL VALUE (PER 100 G): 75 kcal, 2 g protein, 4 g fat, 8 g carbs, 2 g fiber.

GARNISHING TIP: Add a touch of grated lemon zest to enhance the aroma and color.

WARM TENDERNESS — SALAD WITH ROASTED SWEET POTATO AND AVOCADO

DESCRIPTION: This warm salad combines the creamy texture of avocado, the sweetness of roasted sweet potato, and the tangy zest of a light lemon dressing. An ideal choice for a cozy lunch or dinner during colder months.

INGREDIENTS:
- 1 medium sweet potato (about 200 g), cubed
- 1 ripe avocado, sliced
- 3 1/2 ounces (100 g) salad greens (arugula, spinach, or mix)
- 2 tablespoons (30 ml) olive oil (for roasting)
- 1 tablespoon (15 ml) lemon juice
- 1 tablespoon (15 ml) olive oil (for dressing)
- A pinch of salt and freshly ground black pepper
- A few pomegranate seeds (optional)

COOKING TIME: Prep: 10 minutes, Cook: 20 minutes

INSTRUCTIONS:
1. Preheat the oven to 200°C (390°F).
2. Cube the sweet potato and place it on a baking tray. Drizzle with 2 tablespoons of olive oil, sprinkle with salt and pepper, and toss to coat. Roast for 20–25 minutes until soft and golden.
3. Wash and dry the salad greens.
4. Peel and slice the avocado.
5. In a small bowl, mix the lemon juice and the remaining tablespoon of olive oil for the dressing.
6. In a salad bowl, combine the roasted sweet potato, greens, and avocado. Drizzle with the dressing and gently toss to combine.
7. Optionally, garnish with pomegranate seeds for a vibrant touch.

NUTRITIONAL VALUE (PER 100 G): 130 kcal, 2 g protein, 8 g fat, 12 g carbs, 3 g fiber.

GARNISHING TIP: Add a sprinkle of grated lemon zest or a sprig of fresh thyme for an elegant finish.

WINTER RICHES — SALAD WITH ROASTED ROOT VEGETABLES AND POMEGRANATE

DESCRIPTION: This hearty and vibrant salad combines the sweetness of roasted root vegetables, the freshness of pomegranate seeds, and the lightness of a honey-lemon dressing. Perfect for a cozy winter lunch or festive dinner.

INGREDIENTS:
- 1 medium beetroot (about 200 g), cubed
- 1 carrot (about 150 g), cut into sticks
- 1 parsnip or celery root (about 150 g), cubed
- 2 tablespoons (30 ml) olive oil (for roasting)
- 3 1/2 ounces (100 g) salad greens (arugula, spinach, or mix)
- 1/4 cup (40 g) pomegranate seeds
- 2 tablespoons (30 ml) olive oil (for dressing)
- 1 tablespoon (15 ml) lemon juice
- 1 teaspoon (5 ml) honey
- A pinch of salt and freshly ground black pepper

COOKING TIME: Prep: 10 minutes, Cook: 30 minutes

INSTRUCTIONS:
1. Preheat the oven to 200°C (390°F).
2. Chop the root vegetables and place them in a bowl. Drizzle with 2 tablespoons of olive oil, season with salt and pepper, and mix well.
3. Spread the vegetables on a baking tray and roast for 25–30 minutes, flipping occasionally, until soft and slightly caramelized.
4. Wash and dry the salad greens.
5. In a small bowl, combine olive oil, lemon juice, and honey for the dressing.
6. In a salad bowl, combine the salad greens, roasted root vegetables, and pomegranate seeds. Drizzle with the dressing and toss gently to combine.
7. Serve the salad warm, savoring its rich winter flavors.

NUTRITIONAL VALUE (PER 100 G): 110 kcal, 2 g protein, 6 g fat, 10 g carbs, 3 g fiber.

GARNISHING TIP: Add a few fresh mint leaves or a sprinkle of grated lemon zest for added aroma and color.

CRUNCHY WINTER — SALAD WITH PUMPKIN SEEDS AND GREEN CABBAGE

DESCRIPTION: This winter salad combines crunchy green cabbage leaves, aromatic pumpkin seeds, and the lightness of a lemon dressing. A healthy and nutritious dish, perfect for a light lunch or dinner.

INGREDIENTS:
- 2 cups (150 g) finely shredded green cabbage
- 1/4 cup (30 g) toasted pumpkin seeds
- 3 1/2 ounces (100 g) salad greens (arugula or mix)
- 2 tablespoons (30 ml) olive oil
- 1 tablespoon (15 ml) lemon juice
- 1 teaspoon (5 ml) honey
- A pinch of salt and freshly ground black pepper
- A few parsley leaves for garnish (optional)

COOKING TIME: Prep: 10 minutes

INSTRUCTIONS:
1. Finely shred the green cabbage and gently massage it with your hands to soften.
2. Lightly toast the pumpkin seeds in a dry skillet until golden.
3. Wash and dry the salad greens.
4. In a small bowl, mix olive oil, lemon juice, honey, salt, and pepper for the dressing.
5. In a salad bowl, combine the green cabbage, salad greens, and pumpkin seeds. Drizzle with the dressing and toss gently to combine.
6. Garnish the salad with parsley leaves before serving (optional).

NUTRITIONAL VALUE (PER 100 G): 85 kcal, 2 g protein, 5 g fat, 7 g carbs, 2 g fiber.

GARNISHING TIP: Add a few thin slices of radish or a dash of lemon juice for a vibrant touch.

WINTER FOREST WONDER — SALAD WITH PICKLED MUSHROOMS AND ONIONS

DESCRIPTION: This simple and flavorful salad combines the tanginess of pickled mushrooms, the sharpness of onions, and the freshness of greens. A great choice for a winter dinner or as an appetizer on a festive table.

INGREDIENTS:
- 1 cup (150 g) pickled mushrooms (button mushrooms or wild mushrooms)
- 1/2 medium red onion, thinly sliced into rings
- 3 1/2 ounces (100 g) salad greens (arugula, spinach, or mix)
- 2 tablespoons (30 ml) olive oil
- 1 tablespoon (15 ml) apple cider vinegar
- A pinch of salt and freshly ground black pepper
- 1 tablespoon (10 g) finely chopped fresh parsley

COOKING TIME: Prep: 10 minutes

INSTRUCTIONS:
1. Thinly slice the red onion and soak it in cold water for 5 minutes to reduce sharpness. Then pat it dry.
2. Wash and dry the salad greens.
3. In a small bowl, mix olive oil, apple cider vinegar, salt, and pepper to make the dressing.
4. In a salad bowl, combine the salad greens, pickled mushrooms, and onion rings. Drizzle with the dressing and toss gently to combine.
5. Sprinkle the salad with fresh parsley before serving.

NUTRITIONAL VALUE (PER 100 G): 70 kcal, 2 g protein, 4 g fat, 5 g carbs, 1 g fiber.

GARNISHING TIP: Add a few thin lemon slices or sprinkle with finely chopped dill for extra aroma.

WINTER FANTASY — ROASTED BEET AND GOAT CHEESE SALAD

DESCRIPTION: This elegant salad combines the sweetness of roasted beets, the creaminess of goat cheese, and the lightness of a balsamic dressing. It's a perfect addition to a winter dinner or a festive table.

INGREDIENTS:
- 2 medium beets (about 300 g), roasted and diced
- 3 1/2 ounces (100 g) salad greens (arugula or mix)
- 2 ounces (60 g) goat cheese, crumbled
- 1/4 cup (30 g) toasted walnuts
- 2 tablespoons (30 ml) olive oil
- 1 tablespoon (15 ml) balsamic vinegar
- 1 teaspoon (5 ml) honey
- A pinch of salt and freshly ground black pepper

COOKING TIME: Prep: 10 minutes, Cook: 40 minutes

INSTRUCTIONS:
1. Preheat the oven to 200°C (390°F). Peel the beets, wrap them in foil, and roast for 40 minutes or until tender. Let them cool, then cut into cubes.
2. Wash and dry the salad greens.
3. Lightly toast the walnuts in a dry skillet until golden.
4. In a small bowl, mix olive oil, balsamic vinegar, honey, salt, and pepper to make the dressing.
5. In a salad bowl, combine the salad greens, roasted beets, walnuts, and goat cheese. Drizzle with the dressing and toss gently.
6. Serve immediately, enjoying the vibrant flavors and textures.

NUTRITIONAL VALUE (PER 100 G): 110 kcal, 3 g protein, 6 g fat, 9 g carbs, 2 g fiber.

GARNISHING TIP: Add a few pomegranate seeds or some grated orange zest for a bright accent and aroma.

FESTIVE SALADS FOR SPECIAL OCCASIONS: MAGIC ON YOUR TABLE

Holidays are a special time when every moment feels a little magical, homes are filled with light and aromas, and loved ones gather to celebrate together. The festive salads in this section are designed to make any celebration vibrant and memorable. These are more than just salads—they are culinary masterpieces that will amaze your guests and bring a festive atmosphere to your table. Each dish is an opportunity to express love to your loved ones, sharing a part of your creativity and warmth.

In this section, you'll find recipes that can brighten up any holiday, be it Christmas, New Year's, Easter, or any other significant event in your life. We've curated unique flavor combinations that surprise and inspire. Using vibrant ingredients such as pomegranate, citrus, fresh berries, and aromatic herbs transforms each salad into a true work of art. Adding caramelized nuts, cheese, or even exotic fruits lends elegance and richness, emphasizing their festive nature.

Special attention is given not only to the ingredients but also to the presentation of these festive salads. We offer ideas for decorating your salads to create a magical mood at your table: from using edible flowers and greens to arranging colorful components in layers to make each salad a little celebration of its own. For instance, a salad with red cabbage and oranges, garnished with pomegranate seeds and fresh greens, will not only captivate your guests with its appearance but also delight them with its rich flavor that will linger in memory.

Festive salads also feature recipes with unique dressings that make the dishes truly special. Honey-mustard dressing, rosemary-infused vinegar, or orange sauce with a hint of spices add complexity and uniqueness to each salad, creating a festive sensation in every bite. These dressings enhance the taste, bringing out the full range of flavors in each ingredient.

Festive salads are not only delicious but also healthy. Using natural ingredients, fresh fruits, vegetables, nuts, and spices, these dishes please the eye while promoting well-being during the festive season. Light yet satisfying, these salads nourish the body without causing heaviness or fatigue, offering a perfect balance of taste and nutrition. We've ensured that each salad can be easily adapted—by adding protein to make it more filling or altering the dressing to create a new flavor profile.

Let this section be your source of inspiration for creating unforgettable holiday moments. The festive salads featured here are designed to bring warmth and love to your table, foster joy and togetherness, and delight your guests and loved ones with their beauty and taste. Draw inspiration from these recipes, experiment with presentation, add your personal touches, and let every holiday become a culinary wonder!

CHRISTMAS TALE — SALAD WITH RED CABBAGE AND APPLES

DESCRIPTION: This vibrant winter salad combines crunchy red cabbage, the sweetness of apples, and a hint of tartness from apple cider vinegar. A perfect choice for the holiday table to add freshness and bright colors.

INGREDIENTS:
- 2 cups (150 g) finely shredded red cabbage
- 1 large apple (about 200 g), thinly sliced
- 1/4 cup (30 g) toasted walnuts
- 2 tbsp (30 ml) apple cider vinegar
- 1 tbsp (15 ml) olive oil
- 1 tsp (5 ml) honey
- A pinch of salt and freshly ground black pepper
- A few fresh mint leaves for garnish

COOKING TIME: 10 minutes

INSTRUCTIONS:
1. Finely shred the red cabbage and gently massage it with your hands to soften.
2. Slice the apple thinly or cut into cubes.
3. Lightly toast the walnuts in a dry skillet until golden.
4. In a small bowl, mix apple cider vinegar, olive oil, honey, salt, and pepper to make the dressing.
5. In a salad bowl, combine the cabbage, apple, and walnuts. Drizzle with the dressing and toss gently to combine.
6. Garnish the salad with mint leaves before serving.

NUTRITIONAL VALUE (PER 100 G): 90 kcal, 2 g protein, 5 g fat, 9 g carbohydrates, 2 g fiber.

GARNISH TIP: Add a few pomegranate seeds or a drizzle of honey on top for extra sweetness and a festive look.

FESTIVE DELIGHT — SALAD WITH CARAMELIZED NUTS AND GRAPES

DESCRIPTION: This exquisite salad combines the sweetness of grapes, the crunch of caramelized nuts, and the creaminess of soft cheese. A perfect dish for the holiday table to enhance the festive atmosphere.

INGREDIENTS:
- 1 cup (150 g) seedless grapes, halved
- 1/4 cup (30 g) caramelized nuts (walnuts or pecans)
- 3 1/2 oz (100 g) salad greens (arugula, spinach, or mixed greens)
- 2 oz (60 g) cream cheese or soft feta, crumbled
- 2 tbsp (30 ml) olive oil
- 1 tbsp (15 ml) white wine vinegar
- 1 tsp (5 ml) honey
- A pinch of salt and freshly ground black pepper

COOKING TIME: 10 minutes

INSTRUCTIONS:
1. Rinse the grapes and cut them in half.
2. Lightly toast the caramelized nuts in a dry skillet or use pre-made ones.
3. Wash and dry the salad greens.
4. In a small bowl, mix olive oil, white wine vinegar, honey, salt, and pepper to prepare the dressing.
5. In a salad bowl, combine the greens, grapes, caramelized nuts, and cream cheese. Drizzle with the dressing and toss gently.
6. Serve immediately and enjoy the rich flavors and textures.

NUTRITIONAL VALUE (PER 100 G): 120 kcal, 3 g protein, 7 g fat, 10 g carbohydrates, 2 g fiber.

GARNISH TIP: Add a few thin slices of fresh pear or mint leaves for an extra touch of elegance.

NEW YEAR'S SURPRISE — SALAD WITH AVOCADO AND SHRIMP

DESCRIPTION: This sophisticated salad combines the creaminess of avocado, the sweetness of shrimp, and the freshness of a lemon dressing. It will be a highlight on your holiday table and impress guests with its refinement.

INGREDIENTS:
- 1 ripe avocado, diced
- 1 cup (150 g) cooked and peeled shrimp
- 3 1/2 oz (100 g) salad greens (arugula, spinach, or mixed greens)
- 1/4 cup (30 g) toasted pine nuts
- 2 tbsp (30 ml) olive oil
- 1 tbsp (15 ml) lemon juice
- 1 tsp (5 ml) honey
- A pinch of salt and freshly ground black pepper

COOKING TIME: 10 minutes

INSTRUCTIONS:
1. Dice the avocado and drizzle it with lemon juice to prevent browning.
2. Lightly toast the pine nuts in a dry skillet until golden.
3. Wash and dry the salad greens.
4. In a small bowl, mix olive oil, lemon juice, honey, salt, and pepper to prepare the dressing.
5. In a salad bowl, combine the greens, avocado, shrimp, and pine nuts. Drizzle with the dressing and gently toss.
6. Serve the salad immediately, enjoying its freshness and delicacy.

NUTRITIONAL VALUE (PER 100 G): 130 kcal, 6 g protein, 9 g fat, 5 g carbohydrates, 2 g fiber.

GARNISH TIP: Add a few slices of fresh lemon or sprigs of dill for decoration and aroma.

SOPHISTICATED CELEBRATION — SALAD WITH GOAT CHEESE AND FIGS

DESCRIPTION: This elegant salad combines the creaminess of goat cheese, the sweetness of fresh figs, and the nutty flavor of pine nuts. A light honey-balsamic dressing makes it the perfect dish for a festive table.

INGREDIENTS:
- 4 fresh figs, quartered
- 2 oz (60 g) goat cheese, crumbled
- 3 1/2 oz (100 g) salad greens (arugula, spinach, or mixed greens)
- 1/4 cup (30 g) toasted pine nuts
- 2 tbsp (30 ml) olive oil
- 1 tbsp (15 ml) balsamic vinegar
- 1 tsp (5 ml) honey
- A pinch of salt and freshly ground black pepper

COOKING TIME: 10 minutes

INSTRUCTIONS:
1. Quarter the fresh figs.
2. Lightly toast the pine nuts in a dry skillet until golden.
3. Wash and dry the salad greens.
4. In a small bowl, mix olive oil, balsamic vinegar, honey, salt, and pepper for the dressing.
5. In a salad bowl, combine the salad greens, figs, goat cheese, and pine nuts. Drizzle with the dressing and gently toss.
6. Serve the salad immediately, savoring its refined taste.

NUTRITIONAL VALUE (PER 100 G): 120 kcal, 4 g protein, 8 g fat, 7 g carbohydrates, 2 g fiber.

GARNISH TIP: Add a few drops of balsamic glaze or thin slices of fresh figs for an extra touch of sophistication.

ENCHANTED EVENING — HOLIDAY SALAD WITH ROASTED PEAR AND BLUE CHEESE

DESCRIPTION: This elegant salad combines the sweetness of roasted pear, the sharpness of blue cheese, and the nutty crunch of walnuts. A perfect choice for a special evening or festive table.

INGREDIENTS:
- 2 ripe pears, quartered and cored
- 2 oz (60 g) blue cheese, crumbled
- 3 1/2 oz (100 g) salad greens (arugula, spinach, or mixed greens)
- 1/4 cup (30 g) toasted walnuts
- 2 tbsp (30 ml) olive oil (for roasting)
- 1 tbsp (15 ml) balsamic vinegar
- 1 tsp (5 ml) honey
- A pinch of salt and freshly ground black pepper

COOKING TIME: 10 minutes, cooking: 20 minutes

INSTRUCTIONS:
1. Preheat the oven to 200°C (390°F).
2. Quarter the pears, place them on a baking sheet, and drizzle with 1 tablespoon of olive oil. Roast for 15–20 minutes until soft and golden.
3. Lightly toast the walnuts in a dry skillet until aromatic.
4. Wash and dry the salad greens.
5. In a small bowl, mix the remaining 1 tablespoon of olive oil, balsamic vinegar, honey, salt, and pepper to make the dressing.
6. In a salad bowl, combine the salad greens, roasted pears, blue cheese, and walnuts. Drizzle with the dressing and gently toss.
7. Serve the salad immediately, savoring its rich flavor and elegance.

NUTRITIONAL VALUE (PER 100 G): 130 kcal, 4 g protein, 8 g fat, 9 g carbohydrates, 2 g fiber.
GARNISH TIP: Add a few drops of balsamic glaze or thin slices of fresh pear for a refined touch.

SUNNY DELIGHT — SALAD WITH HALLOUMI CHEESE AND GRILLED PEACHES

DESCRIPTION: This vibrant salad combines the tenderness of grilled peaches, the savory taste of halloumi cheese, and the freshness of greens. A light honey-lemon dressing adds sophistication, making it a perfect choice for a festive table or a cozy lunch.

INGREDIENTS:
- 2 ripe peaches, quartered
- 5 oz (150 g) halloumi cheese, sliced
- 3 1/2 oz (100 g) salad greens (arugula, spinach, or mixed greens)
- 1/4 cup (30 g) toasted pine nuts
- 2 tbsp (30 ml) olive oil (for grilling)
- 1 tbsp (15 ml) lemon juice
- 1 tsp (5 ml) honey
- A pinch of salt and freshly ground black pepper

COOKING TIME: preparation: 10 minutes, cooking: 10 minutes

INSTRUCTIONS:
1. Preheat a grill pan over medium heat.
2. Lightly brush the peach slices with olive oil and grill them for 2–3 minutes on each side until golden grill marks appear.
3. Grill the halloumi slices on the same pan for 1–2 minutes on each side until golden.
4. Lightly toast the pine nuts in a dry skillet until aromatic.
5. Wash and dry the salad greens.
6. In a small bowl, mix the remaining olive oil, lemon juice, honey, salt, and pepper for the dressing.
7. In a salad bowl, combine the salad greens, grilled peaches, halloumi, and pine nuts. Drizzle with the dressing and gently toss.
8. Serve the salad immediately, savoring its rich taste and aroma.

NUTRITIONAL VALUE (PER 100 G): 150 kcal, 5 g protein, 9 g fat, 10 g carbohydrates, 1 g fiber.
GARNISH TIP: Garnish the salad with thin slices of fresh lemon or mint leaves for extra freshness.

CITRUS DUCK — SALAD WITH SMOKED DUCK AND ORANGES

DESCRIPTION: This refined salad combines the tenderness of smoked duck, the sweetness of oranges, and the freshness of leafy greens. A light citrus dressing makes it perfect for a special occasion or a festive table.

INGREDIENTS:
- 5 oz (150 g) smoked duck breast, thinly sliced
- 2 oranges, peeled and segmented
- 3 1/2 oz (100 g) salad greens (arugula, spinach, or mixed greens)
- 1/4 cup (30 g) toasted walnuts
- 2 tbsp (30 ml) olive oil
- 1 tbsp (15 ml) orange juice
- 1 tsp (5 ml) honey
- A pinch of salt and freshly ground black pepper
- 1 tsp orange zest for garnish

COOKING TIME: preparation: 10 minutes

INSTRUCTIONS:
1. Slice the smoked duck breast into thin slices.
2. Peel the oranges, remove the white pith, and cut them into segments. Set aside some zest for garnish.
3. Lightly toast the walnuts in a dry skillet until golden.
4. Wash and dry the salad greens.
5. In a small bowl, whisk together the olive oil, orange juice, honey, salt, and pepper for the dressing.
6. In a salad bowl, combine the salad greens, duck slices, orange segments, and toasted walnuts. Drizzle with the dressing and gently toss.
7. Garnish the salad with orange zest before serving.

NUTRITIONAL VALUE (PER 100 G): 180 kcal, 7 g protein, 11 g fat, 12 g carbohydrates, 2 g fiber.

GARNISH TIP: Add a few thin slices of fresh orange or a sprig of thyme for an elegant touch.

TROPICAL FRESHNESS — SALAD WITH GRAPEFRUIT, AVOCADO, AND ARUGULA

DESCRIPTION: This light and refreshing salad combines the creaminess of avocado, the tangy flavor of grapefruit, and the peppery taste of arugula. A delicate citrus dressing highlights the vibrant flavors, making this dish a perfect choice for lunch or dinner.

INGREDIENTS:
- 1 ripe avocado, sliced
- 1 large grapefruit, peeled and segmented
- 3 1/2 oz (100 g) arugula
- 1/4 cup (30 g) toasted pine nuts
- 2 tbsp (30 ml) olive oil
- 1 tbsp (15 ml) grapefruit juice
- 1 tsp (5 ml) honey
- A pinch of salt and freshly ground black pepper
- 1 tsp grated grapefruit zest

COOKING TIME: preparation: 10 minutes

INSTRUCTIONS:
1. Peel the grapefruit, remove the white pith, and segment it.
2. Slice the avocado and drizzle it with a small amount of grapefruit juice to prevent browning.
3. Lightly toast the pine nuts in a dry skillet until golden.
4. Wash and dry the arugula.
5. In a small bowl, mix the olive oil, grapefruit juice, honey, salt, and pepper to make the dressing.
6. In a salad bowl, combine the arugula, grapefruit segments, avocado slices, and toasted pine nuts. Drizzle with the dressing and gently toss.
7. Garnish the salad with grated grapefruit zest before serving.

NUTRITIONAL VALUE (PER 100 G): 130 kcal, 2 g protein, 9 g fat, 10 g carbohydrates, 3 g fiber.

GARNISH TIP: Add a few thin slices of fresh grapefruit or mint leaves to enhance the aroma.

BERRY TENDERNESS — SALAD WITH GRILLED CHICKEN AND RASPBERRIES

DESCRIPTION: This delicate salad combines the juiciness of grilled chicken, the sweetness of raspberries, and the freshness of mixed greens. A light honey mustard dressing enhances the rich flavors, making it a perfect choice for a romantic dinner or a light lunch.

INGREDIENTS:
- 5 oz (150 g) chicken fillet, sliced
- 1/2 cup (75 g) fresh raspberries
- 3 1/2 oz (100 g) mixed salad greens (arugula, spinach, or a mix)
- 1/4 cup (30 g) toasted almond flakes
- 1 tbsp (15 ml) olive oil (for frying)
- 2 tbsp (30 ml) olive oil (for dressing)
- 1 tbsp (15 ml) lemon juice
- 1 tsp (5 ml) honey
- 1/2 tsp Dijon mustard
- A pinch of salt and freshly ground black pepper

COOKING TIME: preparation: 10 minutes, cooking: 15 minutes

INSTRUCTIONS:
1. Heat 1 tablespoon of olive oil in a skillet over medium heat. Grill the chicken fillet until golden on both sides, about 7 minutes, until fully cooked. Let cool, then slice.
2. Wash and dry the salad greens.
3. Toast the almond flakes in a dry skillet until golden brown.
4. In a small bowl, mix 2 tablespoons of olive oil, lemon juice, honey, mustard, salt, and pepper to make the dressing.
5. In a salad bowl, combine the salad greens, raspberries, chicken slices, and almond flakes. Drizzle with the dressing and gently toss.
6. Serve the salad immediately, enjoying its tender flavors and textures.

NUTRITIONAL VALUE (PER 100 G): 140 kcal, 7 g protein, 8 g fat, 9 g carbohydrates, 2 g fiber.

GARNISH TIP: Decorate the salad with a few raspberries and fresh mint leaves for added brightness.

EASTERN TALE — SALAD WITH DATES, ALMONDS, AND YOGURT DRESSING

DESCRIPTION: This refined salad combines the sweetness of dates, the crunch of almonds, and the creaminess of a yogurt dressing. Its sophisticated flavors evoke the aromas of the East, making it perfect for a special dinner or celebration.

INGREDIENTS:
- 1/2 cup (75 g) sliced dates
- 1/4 cup (30 g) toasted almonds
- 3 1/2 oz (100 g) salad greens (arugula, spinach, or a mix)
- 1/4 cup (60 ml) natural yogurt
- 1 tbsp (15 ml) lemon juice
- 1 tsp (5 ml) honey
- 1/4 tsp ground cinnamon
- A pinch of salt and freshly ground black pepper
- A few mint leaves for garnish

COOKING TIME: preparation: 10 minutes

INSTRUCTIONS:
1. Slice the dates into thin strips.
2. Lightly toast the almonds in a dry skillet until golden and chop them into coarse pieces.
3. Wash and dry the salad greens.
4. In a small bowl, mix yogurt, lemon juice, honey, cinnamon, salt, and pepper to make the dressing.
5. In a salad bowl, combine the salad greens, sliced dates, and toasted almonds. Drizzle with the yogurt dressing and gently toss.
6. Garnish the salad with mint leaves before serving.

NUTRITIONAL VALUE (PER 100 G): 120 kcal, 3 g protein, 5 g fat, 15 g carbohydrates, 2 g fiber.

DECORATION TIP: Add a sprinkle of grated orange zest or a few pomegranate seeds for a vibrant accent and extra sweetness.

FESTIVE GLOW — SALAD WITH GRAPES, NUTS, AND BRIE CHEESE

DESCRIPTION: This sophisticated salad combines the sweetness of grapes, the creaminess of Brie cheese, and the crunch of walnuts. A light honey-mustard dressing makes it a perfect choice for a holiday table.

INGREDIENTS:
- 1 cup (150 g) seedless grapes, halved
- 3 1/2 oz (100 g) Brie cheese, sliced
- 3 1/2 oz (100 g) salad greens (arugula, spinach, or a mix)
- 1/4 cup (30 g) toasted walnuts
- 2 tbsp (30 ml) olive oil
- 1 tbsp (15 ml) lemon juice
- 1 tsp (5 ml) honey
- 1/2 tsp Dijon mustard
- A pinch of salt and freshly ground black pepper

COOKING TIME: preparation: 10 minutes

INSTRUCTIONS:
1. Wash the grapes and cut them in half.
2. Slice the Brie cheese into pieces.
3. Lightly toast the walnuts in a dry skillet until golden.
4. Wash and dry the salad greens.
5. In a small bowl, whisk together olive oil, lemon juice, honey, mustard, salt, and pepper to make the dressing.
6. In a salad bowl, combine the salad greens, grapes, Brie cheese, and toasted walnuts. Drizzle with the dressing and gently toss.
7. Serve the salad immediately, savoring its delicate flavors.

NUTRITIONAL VALUE (PER 100 G): 140 kcal, 5 g protein, 9 g fat, 10 g carbohydrates, 2 g fiber.

DECORATION TIP: Garnish the salad with a few whole grapes and fresh mint leaves for a festive look.

CHRISTMAS MIRACLE — SALAD WITH MANDARINS, WALNUTS, AND YOGURT DRESSING

DESCRIPTION: This festive salad combines the sweetness of mandarins, the crunch of walnuts, and the creaminess of a yogurt dressing. Its light and refreshing flavors make it perfect for a Christmas dinner or holiday lunch.

INGREDIENTS:
- 2 mandarins, peeled and separated into segments
- 3 1/2 oz (100 g) salad greens (arugula, spinach, or a mix)
- 1/4 cup (30 g) toasted walnuts
- 1/4 cup (60 ml) plain yogurt
- 1 tbsp (15 ml) lemon juice
- 1 tsp (5 ml) honey
- A pinch of salt and freshly ground black pepper
- 1 tsp grated mandarin zest for aroma

COOKING TIME: preparation: 10 minutes

INSTRUCTIONS:
1. Peel the mandarins and separate them into segments. Set aside some zest for garnish.
2. Lightly toast the walnuts in a dry skillet until golden.
3. Wash and dry the salad greens.
4. In a small bowl, whisk together yogurt, lemon juice, honey, salt, and pepper to make the dressing.
5. In a salad bowl, combine the salad greens, mandarin segments, and toasted walnuts. Drizzle with the dressing and gently toss.
6. Garnish the salad with mandarin zest before serving.

NUTRITIONAL VALUE (PER 100 G): 90 kcal, 2 g protein, 5 g fat, 9 g carbohydrates, 2 g fiber.

DECORATION TIP: Add a few pomegranate seeds or a sprig of fresh mint for a bright accent and festive appearance.

PROTEIN SALADS: POWER AND ENERGY FOR AN ACTIVE LIFE

Protein salads are not just meals; they are a source of energy that fuels us for an active lifestyle. In this section, you'll find recipes designed to meet your body's need for high-quality protein while maintaining the lightness and freshness essential to your diet. These salads are perfect for those who strive for an active lifestyle, care about their muscles, and want to stay in harmony with nature by using natural and healthy ingredients.

The **protein salads** featured here incorporate a variety of protein sources: from plant-based options like chickpeas, beans, and quinoa to more traditional choices like chicken breast, fish, eggs, and cheese. The combination of these ingredients with seasonal vegetables and unique dressings creates rich, flavorful, and nutritious dishes that provide a sense of fullness while supplying your body with essential amino acids and vitamins. For example, a salad with chicken breast, avocado, and spinach is rich in both protein and healthy fats, while a quinoa and chickpea salad with vegetables offers a vegetarian option packed with plant-based proteins and fiber.

A standout feature of protein salads is their versatility: they can serve as a light lunch or a hearty dinner. These dishes are suitable not only for athletes and fitness enthusiasts but for anyone seeking to incorporate balanced, filling, and healthy meals into their diet. Dressings play a crucial role in flavor harmony—light lemon-based, honey-mustard, or olive oil-based dressings complement each salad and enhance the taste of the main ingredients.

Each recipe is a small culinary adventure that unveils the magic of protein in harmony with nature's bounty. The protein salads in this section will help you feel energetic, strong, and ready for new achievements. Let these recipes inspire you to create delicious and nutritious dishes that provide energy and satisfaction while remaining light and sophisticated.

CITRUS BOOST — SALAD WITH CHICKEN, AVOCADO, AND GRAPEFRUIT

DESCRIPTION: This refreshing salad combines the juiciness of grapefruit, the tenderness of chicken, and the creamy texture of avocado. A light citrus dressing enhances the harmony of flavors, making this dish perfect for lunch or dinner.

INGREDIENTS:
- 5 oz (150 g) cooked or grilled chicken breast, sliced
- 1 large grapefruit, peeled and segmented
- 1 ripe avocado, sliced
- 3 1/2 oz (100 g) salad greens (arugula, spinach, or mix)
- 2 tbsp (30 ml) olive oil
- 1 tbsp (15 ml) grapefruit juice
- 1 tsp (5 ml) honey
- Pinch of salt and freshly ground black pepper
- A few fresh mint leaves for garnish

COOKING TIME: 10 minutes

INSTRUCTIONS:
1. Slice the chicken breast.
2. Peel the grapefruit, remove the white pith, and segment it.
3. Slice the avocado and drizzle it with a little grapefruit juice to prevent browning.
4. Wash and dry the salad greens.
5. In a small bowl, combine olive oil, grapefruit juice, honey, salt, and pepper to make the dressing.
6. In a salad bowl, combine the salad greens, chicken, grapefruit, and avocado. Drizzle with the dressing and toss gently.
7. Garnish the salad with fresh mint leaves before serving.

NUTRITIONAL VALUE (PER 100 G): 140 kcal, 8 g protein, 9 g fat, 6 g carbohydrates, 2 g fiber.

GARNISH TIP: Add a few thin slices of grapefruit or sprinkle grated zest on top for extra brightness and aroma.

SEA BREEZE — TUNA WITH BEANS AND FRESH GREENS

DESCRIPTION: This nutritious and light salad combines the rich flavor of tuna, the creaminess of beans, and the freshness of greens. A light lemon-olive dressing makes it an excellent choice for lunch or dinner.

INGREDIENTS:
- 1 can (150 g) of tuna in water, drained
- 1 cup (150 g) of canned white beans, rinsed and dried
- 3 1/2 oz (100 g) salad greens (arugula, spinach, or mix)
- 1/4 cup (30 g) toasted pumpkin or sunflower seeds
- 2 tbsp (30 ml) olive oil
- 1 tbsp (15 ml) lemon juice
- 1 tsp (5 ml) Dijon mustard
- Pinch of salt and freshly ground black pepper

COOKING TIME: 10 minutes

INSTRUCTIONS:
1. Drain the canned tuna and flake it into small pieces with a fork.
2. Rinse the beans under cold water and pat them dry.
3. Lightly toast the pumpkin or sunflower seeds in a dry skillet until golden brown.
4. Wash and dry the salad greens.
5. In a small bowl, mix olive oil, lemon juice, mustard, salt, and pepper to prepare the dressing.
6. In a salad bowl, combine the salad greens, beans, tuna, and toasted seeds. Drizzle with the dressing and toss gently.
7. Serve the salad immediately and enjoy its rich flavor.

NUTRITIONAL VALUE (PER 100 G): 150 kcal, 12 g protein, 7 g fat, 8 g carbohydrates, 2 g fiber.

GARNISH TIP: Garnish the salad with lemon slices or a sprig of fresh dill for extra brightness.

PROTEIN HARMONY — QUINOA, EGG, AND CHICKPEA SALAD

DESCRIPTION: This nutritious salad combines the softness of quinoa, the creamy texture of eggs, and the heartiness of chickpeas. A light lemon-mustard dressing makes it a balanced choice for lunch or dinner.

INGREDIENTS:
- 1/2 cup (90 g) cooked quinoa
- 1 cup (150 g) canned chickpeas, rinsed and dried
- 2 boiled eggs, sliced
- 3 1/2 oz (100 g) salad greens (arugula, spinach, or mix)
- 1/4 cup (30 g) toasted pumpkin seeds
- 2 tbsp (30 ml) olive oil
- 1 tbsp (15 ml) lemon juice
- 1 tsp (5 ml) Dijon mustard
- Pinch of salt and freshly ground black pepper

COOKING TIME: 10 minutes

INSTRUCTIONS:
1. Cook the quinoa according to package instructions and let it cool.
2. Rinse the chickpeas under cold water and pat them dry.
3. Lightly toast the pumpkin seeds in a dry skillet until golden brown.
4. Wash and dry the salad greens.
5. In a small bowl, mix olive oil, lemon juice, mustard, salt, and pepper to prepare the dressing.
6. In a salad bowl, combine the salad greens, quinoa, chickpeas, sliced eggs, and toasted pumpkin seeds. Drizzle with the dressing and toss gently.
7. Serve the salad immediately, enjoying its balanced taste and texture.

NUTRITIONAL VALUE (PER 100 G): 160 kcal, 7 g protein, 8 g fat, 14 g carbohydrates, 3 g fiber.
GARNISH TIP: Garnish the salad with lemon slices or fresh parsley leaves for extra aroma and color.

CRANBERRY DELIGHT — TURKEY SALAD WITH CRANBERRY SAUCE

DESCRIPTION: This festive salad combines the tender meat of turkey, the sweetness of cranberry sauce, and the freshness of salad greens. A light honey-mustard accent in the dressing makes it a balanced dish, perfect for a special occasion.

INGREDIENTS:
- 5 oz (150 g) cooked turkey breast, sliced
- 1/4 cup (60 ml) cranberry sauce
- 3 1/2 oz (100 g) salad greens (arugula, spinach, or mix)
- 1/4 cup (30 g) toasted walnuts
- 2 tbsp (30 ml) olive oil
- 1 tbsp (15 ml) lemon juice
- 1 tsp (5 ml) honey
- 1/2 tsp Dijon mustard
- Pinch of salt and freshly ground black pepper

COOKING TIME: 10 minutes

INSTRUCTIONS:
1. Slice the cooked turkey breast into thin pieces.
2. Lightly toast the walnuts in a dry skillet until golden brown.
3. Wash and dry the salad greens.
4. In a small bowl, mix olive oil, lemon juice, honey, mustard, salt, and pepper for the dressing.
5. In a salad bowl, combine the salad greens, turkey slices, and toasted walnuts. Drizzle with the dressing and toss gently.
6. Top the salad with a spoonful of cranberry sauce and serve immediately.

NUTRITIONAL VALUE (PER 100 G): 150 kcal, 9 g protein, 8 g fat, 10 g carbohydrates, 2 g fiber.
GARNISH TIP: Add some fresh cranberries or mint leaves for extra accent and a festive look.

SEA FRESHNESS — SHRIMP AND AVOCADO SALAD

DESCRIPTION: This refreshing salad combines tender shrimp, the creamy texture of avocado, and the spiciness of salad greens. A light lemon dressing accentuates the natural flavors, making it the perfect choice for a light dinner or lunch.

INGREDIENTS:
- 5 oz (150 g) cooked and peeled shrimp
- 1 ripe avocado, sliced
- 3 1/2 oz (100 g) salad greens (arugula, spinach, or mixed)
- 1/4 cup (30 g) toasted pine nuts
- 2 tbsp (30 ml) olive oil
- 1 tbsp (15 ml) lemon juice
- 1 tsp (5 ml) honey
- Pinch of salt and freshly ground black pepper

COOKING TIME: 10 minutes

INSTRUCTIONS:
1. If the shrimp are not prepped, peel them and pat dry.
2. Slice the avocado and drizzle with a little lemon juice to prevent browning.
3. Lightly toast the pine nuts in a dry skillet until golden brown.
4. Wash and dry the salad greens.
5. In a small bowl, mix the olive oil, lemon juice, honey, salt, and pepper for the dressing.
6. In a salad bowl, combine the salad greens, shrimp, avocado, and pine nuts. Drizzle with the dressing and toss gently.
7. Serve the salad immediately, enjoying its refined taste.

NUTRITIONAL VALUE (PER 100 G): 130 kcal, 6 g protein, 8 g fat, 5 g carbohydrates, 2 g fiber.

GARNISH TIP: Decorate the salad with thin lemon slices or fresh mint leaves for added freshness.

TERIYAKI INSPIRATION — BEEF SALAD WITH TERIYAKI SAUCE

DESCRIPTION: This vibrant salad combines juicy beef, the rich flavor of teriyaki sauce, and the freshness of greens. A great choice for lovers of Eastern cuisine, it's perfect for dinner or lunch.

INGREDIENTS:
- 5 oz (150 g) beef steak, sliced
- 3 1/2 oz (100 g) salad greens (arugula, spinach, or mix)
- 1/4 cup (30 g) carrot, julienned
- 1/4 cup (30 g) toasted sesame seeds
- 2 tbsp (30 ml) teriyaki sauce
- 1 tbsp (15 ml) olive oil (for frying)
- 1 tbsp (15 ml) lemon juice
- Pinch of salt and freshly ground black pepper

COOKING TIME: preparation: 10 minutes, cooking: 15 minutes

INSTRUCTIONS:
1. Heat a skillet over medium heat and add olive oil. Fry the beef slices to your desired doneness (about 2–3 minutes per side for medium). At the end, add teriyaki sauce to coat the meat.
2. Transfer the beef to a plate and allow it to cool slightly.
3. Wash and dry the salad greens.
4. Julienne the carrot or use a special grater.
5. In a small bowl, mix lemon juice, salt, and pepper for a light dressing.
6. In a salad bowl, combine the greens, carrot, and sesame seeds. Drizzle with the dressing and toss gently.
7. Top the salad with teriyaki-coated beef slices.
8. Serve immediately, enjoying the rich flavor of the salad.

NUTRITIONAL VALUE (PER 100 G): 170 kcal, 10 g protein, 9 g fat, 8 g carbohydrates, 2 g fiber.

GARNISH TIP: Drizzle with extra teriyaki sauce and garnish with cilantro leaves for an Eastern touch.

HOMELY COMFORT — BUCKWHEAT, EGG, AND HERB SALAD

DESCRIPTION: This nourishing and cozy salad combines the richness of buckwheat, the tenderness of boiled eggs, and the freshness of greens. A light yogurt dressing makes the dish balanced and perfect for lunch or dinner.
INGREDIENTS:
- 1/2 cup (90 g) cooked buckwheat
- 2 boiled eggs, sliced
- 3 1/2 oz (100 g) salad greens (spinach, dill, parsley, or mix)
- 1/4 cup (60 ml) plain yogurt
- 1 tbsp (15 ml) lemon juice
- 1 tsp (5 ml) olive oil
- Pinch of salt and freshly ground black pepper
- 1 tbsp (10 g) finely chopped green onions for garnish

COOKING TIME: 10 minutes
INSTRUCTIONS:
1. Cook the buckwheat according to the package instructions and let it cool.
2. Slice the boiled eggs.
3. Wash and dry the salad greens.
4. In a small bowl, mix the yogurt, lemon juice, olive oil, salt, and pepper for the dressing.
5. In a salad bowl, combine the buckwheat, salad greens, and eggs. Drizzle with the dressing and gently toss.
6. Garnish the salad with finely chopped green onions before serving.

NUTRITIONAL VALUE (PER 100 G): 130 kcal, 5 g protein, 5 g fat, 15 g carbohydrates, 2 g fiber.
GARNISH TIP: Add a few slices of fresh cucumber or sprinkle with grated Parmesan for a more interesting flavor.

PROTEIN DELICACY — CHICKEN, BROCCOLI, AND ALMOND SALAD

DESCRIPTION: This nutritious salad combines the tenderness of chicken, the crunch of broccoli, and the nutty flavor of almonds. A light lemon-yogurt dressing makes the dish balanced, perfect for a hearty lunch or dinner.
INGREDIENTS:
- 5 oz (150 g) boiled or roasted chicken breast, sliced
- 1 cup (150 g) broccoli, cut into small florets
- 1/4 cup (30 g) toasted almonds (sliced or coarsely chopped)
- 3 1/2 oz (100 g) salad greens (arugula, spinach, or mix)
- 1/4 cup (60 ml) plain yogurt
- 1 tbsp (15 ml) lemon juice
- 1 tsp (5 ml) honey
- Pinch of salt and freshly ground black pepper

COOKING TIME: preparation: 10 minutes, cooking: 15 minutes
INSTRUCTIONS:
1. Boil the broccoli in boiling water for 2–3 minutes until tender but still crisp. Cool it by rinsing with cold water and pat dry.
2. Slice the chicken breast.
3. Lightly toast the almonds in a dry skillet until golden.
4. Wash and dry the salad greens.
5. In a small bowl, mix the yogurt, lemon juice, honey, salt, and pepper to make the dressing.
6. In a salad bowl, combine the salad greens, broccoli, chicken, and almonds. Drizzle with the dressing and gently toss.
7. Serve immediately and enjoy its rich taste and texture.

NUTRITIONAL VALUE (PER 100 G): 140 kcal, 10 g protein, 6 g fat, 10 g carbohydrates, 2 g fiber.
GARNISH TIP: Garnish with grated lemon zest or a few thin slices of radish for a bright accent.

CITRUS SALMON — SALAD WITH SALMON AND ORANGE SAUCE

DESCRIPTION: This refined salad combines the rich flavor of salmon, the sweetness of oranges, and the freshness of salad greens. The orange dressing adds brightness and harmony, making it an ideal choice for a festive dinner or a light lunch.

INGREDIENTS:
- 5 oz (150 g) baked or smoked salmon, sliced
- 1 orange, peeled and sliced
- 3 1/2 oz (100 g) salad greens (arugula, spinach, or mix)
- 1/4 cup (30 g) toasted pumpkin seeds
- 2 tbsp (30 ml) orange juice
- 1 tbsp (15 ml) olive oil
- 1 tsp (5 ml) honey
- Pinch of salt and freshly ground black pepper
- 1 tsp grated orange zest for garnish

COOKING TIME: 10 minutes

INSTRUCTIONS:
1. Slice the salmon into thin pieces.
2. Peel the orange, remove the white pith, and slice it into wedges.
3. Lightly toast the pumpkin seeds in a dry skillet until golden.
4. Wash and dry the salad greens.
5. In a small bowl, mix the orange juice, olive oil, honey, salt, and pepper to make the dressing.
6. In a salad bowl, combine the salad greens, salmon, orange slices, and pumpkin seeds. Drizzle with the dressing and gently toss.
7. Garnish the salad with grated orange zest before serving.

NUTRITIONAL VALUE (PER 100 G): 150 kcal, 10 g protein, 8 g fat, 8 g carbohydrates, 2 g fiber

GARNISH TIP: Add a few thin slices of fresh orange or fresh mint leaves for extra elegance.

ENERGY GREENS — SALAD WITH LENTILS, EGG, AND SPINACH

DESCRIPTION: This nourishing salad combines the heartiness of lentils, the tenderness of boiled eggs, and the freshness of spinach. The light lemon-mustard dressing accentuates the rich flavors, making the dish perfect for a balanced lunch or dinner.

INGREDIENTS:
- 1/2 cup (90 g) cooked green or brown lentils
- 2 boiled eggs, sliced
- 3 1/2 oz (100 g) fresh spinach
- 1/4 cup (30 g) toasted sunflower seeds
- 2 tbsp (30 ml) olive oil
- 1 tbsp (15 ml) lemon juice
- 1 tsp (5 ml) Dijon mustard
- Pinch of salt and freshly ground black pepper

COOKING TIME: 10 minutes

INSTRUCTIONS:
1. Cook the lentils according to the package instructions and let them cool.
2. Slice the boiled eggs.
3. Lightly toast the sunflower seeds in a dry skillet until golden.
4. Wash and dry the spinach.
5. In a small bowl, mix olive oil, lemon juice, mustard, salt, and pepper for the dressing.
6. In a salad bowl, combine the spinach, lentils, eggs, and toasted sunflower seeds. Drizzle with the dressing and gently toss.
7. Serve the salad immediately, enjoying its rich flavors.

NUTRITIONAL VALUE (PER 100 G): 130 kcal, 7 g protein, 6 g fat, 10 g carbohydrates, 3 g fiber

GARNISH TIP: Garnish the salad with thin lemon slices or fresh parsley leaves for extra freshness.

SPICY TOUCH — SALAD WITH ROAST BEEF AND HORSERADISH DRESSING

DESCRIPTION: This refined salad combines the tenderness of roast beef, the sharpness of horseradish dressing, and the freshness of salad greens. Its rich flavor and subtle heat make it an ideal choice for dinner or a festive table.

INGREDIENTS:
- 5 oz (150 g) thinly sliced roast beef
- 3 1/2 oz (100 g) salad greens (arugula, spinach, or mix)
- 1/4 cup (30 g) toasted pumpkin seeds
- 1 small red onion, thinly sliced into rings
- 2 tbsp (30 ml) olive oil
- 1 tbsp (15 ml) lemon juice
- 1 tsp (5 ml) grated horseradish (or horseradish sauce)
- 1 tsp (5 ml) honey
- Pinch of salt and freshly ground black pepper

COOKING TIME: 10 minutes

INSTRUCTIONS:
1. Slice the roast beef into thin pieces.
2. Lightly toast the pumpkin seeds in a dry skillet until golden.
3. Wash and dry the salad greens.
4. Slice the red onion into thin rings.
5. In a small bowl, mix olive oil, lemon juice, grated horseradish, honey, salt, and pepper for the dressing.
6. In a salad bowl, combine the salad greens, roast beef, red onion, and pumpkin seeds. Drizzle with the dressing and gently toss.
7. Serve the salad immediately, enjoying its rich flavor.

NUTRITIONAL VALUE (PER 100 G): 150 kcal, 9 g protein, 8 g fat, 8 g carbohydrates, 2 g fiber

GARNISH TIP: Garnish the salad with fresh lemon slices or small sprigs of dill for an elegant touch.

GREEK INSPIRATION — SALAD WITH CHICKEN, FETA, AND OLIVES

DESCRIPTION: This vibrant salad combines the tenderness of chicken, the salty flavor of feta, and the richness of olives. A light lemon dressing makes it the perfect choice for a refreshing lunch or dinner.

INGREDIENTS:
- 5 oz (150 g) boiled or grilled chicken breast, sliced
- 3 1/2 oz (100 g) salad greens (arugula, spinach, or mix)
- 1/4 cup (40 g) crumbled feta
- 1/4 cup (30 g) pitted olives, sliced
- 1 small cucumber, sliced into half-moons
- 1/4 red onion, thinly sliced into rings
- 2 tbsp (30 ml) olive oil
- 1 tbsp (15 ml) lemon juice
- 1 tsp (5 ml) Dijon mustard
- Pinch of salt and freshly ground black pepper

COOKING TIME: 10 minutes

INSTRUCTIONS:
1. Slice the chicken breast.
2. Wash and dry the salad greens.
3. Slice the cucumber into half-moons and the red onion into thin rings.
4. In a small bowl, mix olive oil, lemon juice, mustard, salt, and pepper for the dressing.
5. In a salad bowl, combine the salad greens, chicken, feta, olives, cucumber, and red onion. Drizzle with the dressing and gently toss.
6. Serve the salad immediately, enjoying its refreshing taste.

NUTRITIONAL VALUE (PER 100 G): 150 kcal, 10 g protein, 8 g fat, 6 g carbohydrates, 2 g fiber

GARNISH TIP: Garnish with lemon slices or fresh oregano sprigs for a Greek-inspired touch.

VEGAN SALADS: HARMONY WITH NATURE AND PURE FLAVORS

Vegan salads are a celebration for those who appreciate the natural power of plants and seek to create harmony with nature. In this section, you will find recipes fully based on nature's gifts: fresh vegetables, fruits, greens, and grains, which provide incredible richness and flavor to the dishes. Vegan salads are not just food, they are a way to express love for nature, care for your body, and respect for the world around you. They are perfect not only for those who follow a vegan lifestyle but also for anyone who seeks to enrich their diet with healthy and nutritious dishes.

The main ingredients of vegan salads are green leaves, juicy fruits, various root vegetables, and nuts, which fill each salad with its unique texture and richness. In these recipes, you'll find combinations that surprise and inspire: for example, a salad with roasted sweet potatoes and chickpeas, which is not only hearty but also has a pleasant nutty flavor, or a salad with pomegranate and orange, adding freshness and a light tang. The use of various spices and herbs like coriander, basil, and thyme allows for creating unique aromas that enhance the flavors of the ingredients, giving each salad its individuality.

Vegan salads can be light or hearty and are suitable for any occasion — whether it's a picnic lunch, a post-workout dinner, or a festive table. These dishes fill the body with all the necessary elements, from vitamins and minerals to healthy fats and proteins found in grains, legumes, and nuts. Light lemon, honey, or tahini dressings complement the textures and provide a harmonious flavor, making each salad a true gastronomic delight.

Preparing vegan salads is a creative process, where each ingredient plays an important role, contributing to the symphony of flavors and aromas. Garnish the dishes with edible flowers, use various greens to create contrast, and add some nuts or seeds for crunch — and your salad will turn into a true masterpiece. Let this section inspire you to create dishes that are not only healthy and nutritious but also fill you with energy, help you feel closer to nature, and delight in their simplicity and beauty. Vegan salads are a way to give yourself health, lightness, and enjoyment in every meal.

NATURAL ENERGY— CHICKPEA AND FRESH VEGETABLE SALAD

DESCRIPTION: This bright and nutritious salad combines the tenderness of chickpeas, the freshness of vegetables, and the rich flavor of a lemon dressing. It is a light and balanced dish, perfect for lunch or a snack.

INGREDIENTS:
- 1 cup (150 g) canned chickpeas, rinsed and drained
- 1 medium cucumber, diced
- 1 tomato, diced
- 1/4 red onion, finely diced
- 3 1/2 oz (100 g) salad greens (arugula, spinach, or mixed greens)
- 1/4 cup (30 g) roasted sunflower seeds
- 2 tbsp (30 ml) olive oil
- 1 tbsp (15 ml) lemon juice
- 1 tsp (5 ml) honey
- A pinch of salt and freshly ground black pepper

COOKING TIME: Preparation: 10 minutes

INSTRUCTIONS:
1. Rinse the chickpeas under cold water, drain, and place in a large salad bowl.
2. Dice the cucumber and tomato, and add them to the chickpeas.
3. Finely dice the red onion and add it to the other ingredients.
4. Rinse and dry the salad greens, then add them to the bowl.
5. Lightly toast the sunflower seeds in a dry skillet until golden.
6. In a small bowl, mix the olive oil, lemon juice, honey, salt, and pepper for the dressing.
7. Pour the dressing over the salad and gently toss to combine.
8. Serve immediately, enjoying the freshness and harmony of the flavors.

NUTRITIONAL VALUE (PER 100 G): 140 kcal, 5 g protein, 7 g fat, 12 g carbohydrates, 3 g fiber

DECORATION TIP: Garnish with thin slices of lemon or fresh parsley leaves for added freshness.

MEDITERRANEAN INSPIRATION — TABOULI WITH HERBS AND LEMON

DESCRIPTION: This classic tabbouleh salad combines fresh herbs, the aroma of lemon, and the richness of bulgur. Light and refreshing, it's perfect as a side dish or a light snack.

INGREDIENTS:
- 1/2 cup (90 g) cooked bulgur
- 1 large bunch of parsley, finely chopped (about 50 g)
- 1/4 cup (15 g) fresh mint, finely chopped
- 1 medium tomato, finely diced
- 1 small cucumber, diced
- 2 tbsp (30 ml) olive oil
- 2 tbsp (30 ml) lemon juice
- A pinch of salt and freshly ground black pepper
- 1 tsp grated lemon zest for aroma

COOKING TIME: Preparation: 15 minutes

INSTRUCTIONS:
1. Cook the bulgur according to the package instructions and allow it to cool.
2. Finely chop the parsley and mint.
3. Dice the tomato and cucumber.
4. In a large salad bowl, combine the bulgur, chopped herbs, tomato, and cucumber.
5. In a small bowl, mix olive oil, lemon juice, zest, salt, and pepper for the dressing.
6. Pour the dressing over the salad and gently toss to combine.
7. Serve immediately, or refrigerate before serving for a more intense flavor.

NUTRITIONAL VALUE (PER 100 G): 110 kcal, 3 g protein, 5 g fat, 13 g carbohydrates, 3 g fiber

DECORATION TIP: Garnish with lemon wedges or extra mint leaves for a vibrant accent.

LEMON FRESHNESS – QUINOA SALAD WITH AVOCADO AND LEMON DRESSING

DESCRIPTION: This light and nourishing salad combines the delicate flavor of avocado, the nutty texture of quinoa, and a refreshing lemon dressing. It's the perfect choice for lunch or a light dinner.

INGREDIENTS:
- 1/2 cup (90 g) cooked quinoa
- 1 ripe avocado, diced
- 1/2 cup (75 g) cherry tomatoes, halved
- 3 1/2 oz (100 g) salad greens (arugula, spinach, or mix)
- 2 tbsp (30 ml) olive oil
- 1 tbsp (15 ml) lemon juice
- 1 tsp (5 ml) honey
- 1 tsp grated lemon zest
- A pinch of salt and freshly ground pepper

COOKING TIME: Preparation: 10 minutes

INSTRUCTIONS:
1. Cook the quinoa according to the package instructions and let it cool.
2. Dice the avocado and drizzle it with a little lemon juice to prevent browning.
3. Halve the cherry tomatoes.
4. Rinse and dry the salad greens.
5. In a small bowl, mix olive oil, lemon juice, honey, zest, salt, and pepper for the dressing.
6. In a salad bowl, combine quinoa, salad greens, avocado, and tomatoes. Drizzle with dressing and gently toss to combine.
7. Serve immediately, enjoying the freshness and harmony of flavors.

NUTRITIONAL VALUE (PER 100 G): 140 kcal, 4 g protein, 7 g fat, 13 g carbohydrates, 3 g fiber

DECORATION TIP: Garnish with thin lemon slices or an extra pinch of lemon zest to enhance the aroma.

VEGETABLE WARMTH – ROASTED VEGETABLE SALAD WITH TAHINI

DESCRIPTION: This hearty and flavorful salad combines the sweetness of roasted vegetables and the creamy texture of tahini. The perfect choice for a warm lunch or cozy dinner.

INGREDIENTS:
- 1 medium eggplant, diced
- 1 small sweet potato (batata), diced
- 1 red bell pepper, sliced into strips
- 1 red onion, sliced into wedges
- 2 tbsp (30 ml) olive oil
- 3 1/2 oz (100 g) salad greens (arugula or mix)
- 2 tbsp (30 ml) tahini
- 1 tbsp (15 ml) lemon juice
- 1 tsp (5 ml) honey
- 1 tsp cumin
- A pinch of salt and freshly ground pepper

COOKING TIME: Preparation: 10 minutes, Cooking: 25 minutes

INSTRUCTIONS:
Preheat the oven to 200°C (390°F).
Arrange the eggplant, sweet potato, red bell pepper, and onion on a baking sheet. Drizzle with olive oil, sprinkle with cumin, salt, and pepper. Toss to coat.
Roast the vegetables for 20–25 minutes, until tender and slightly golden, stirring occasionally.
While the vegetables are roasting, rinse and dry the salad greens.
In a small bowl, mix tahini, lemon juice, honey, salt, and pepper. If the dressing is too thick, add a little water to reach the desired consistency.
In a salad bowl, combine the roasted vegetables and salad greens. Drizzle with the tahini dressing and gently toss.
Serve the salad warm, enjoying its rich flavor.

NUTRITIONAL VALUE (PER 100 G): 120 kcal, 3 g protein, 6 g fat, 13 g carbohydrates, 3 g fiber

DECORATION TIP: Garnish with a sprinkle of sesame seeds or fresh parsley leaves for added aroma and texture.

TOFU AND GREENS – LIGHTNESS AND FRESHNESS

DESCRIPTION: This light and nutritious salad combines the delicate taste of tofu, the freshness of greens, and the tang of a lemon dressing. It's a great choice for lunch or a light dinner, especially for those following a plant-based diet.

INGREDIENTS:
- 5 oz (150 g) tofu, diced
- 3 1/2 oz (100 g) salad greens (arugula, spinach, or mixed greens)
- 1/4 cup (30 g) roasted pumpkin seeds
- 1/2 small cucumber, sliced into half-moons
- 1 tbsp (15 ml) soy sauce
- 1 tbsp (15 ml) olive oil (for frying tofu)
- 2 tbsp (30 ml) lemon juice
- 1 tsp (5 ml) honey (or agave syrup for vegans)
- A pinch of salt and freshly ground pepper

COOKING TIME: Preparation: 10 minutes, Cooking: 5 minutes

INSTRUCTIONS:
1. Heat a skillet over medium heat and fry the tofu in olive oil until golden and crispy, about 3–5 minutes. Add the soy sauce at the end, stir, and cool.
2. Rinse and dry the salad greens.
3. Slice the cucumber into half-moons.
4. Lightly toast the pumpkin seeds in a dry skillet until golden.
5. In a small bowl, mix the lemon juice, honey (or agave syrup), salt, and pepper for the dressing.
6. In a salad bowl, combine the salad greens, fried tofu, cucumber, and pumpkin seeds. Drizzle with the dressing and toss gently.
7. Serve immediately, enjoying its freshness and lightness.

NUTRITIONAL VALUE (PER 100 G): 120 kcal, 7 g protein, 6 g fat, 8 g carbohydrates, 2 g fiber

DECORATION TIP: Garnish with lemon slices or sprinkle with sesame seeds for added texture and flavor.

SEA INSPIRATION – SEAWEED SALAD WITH SESAME DRESSING

DESCRIPTION: This unique and nutritious salad combines the freshness of seaweed with the rich flavor of sesame dressing. Light and healthy, it's a perfect choice for fans of Eastern cuisine.

INGREDIENTS:
- 1 cup (150 g) seaweed (wakame or chuka)
- 1/4 cup (30 g) thinly sliced cucumber
- 1 tbsp (15 g) toasted sesame seeds
- 1 tbsp (15 ml) soy sauce
- 1 tbsp (15 ml) rice vinegar
- 1 tsp (5 ml) sesame oil
- 1/2 tsp honey (or agave syrup for vegans)
- A pinch of red pepper (optional)

COOKING TIME: Preparation: 10 minutes

INSTRUCTIONS:
1. Rinse the seaweed under cold water and pat dry. If using dried seaweed, soak it in water for 5–7 minutes, then squeeze out any excess water.
2. Slice the cucumber into thin strips.
3. In a small bowl, combine soy sauce, rice vinegar, sesame oil, honey, and, if desired, a pinch of red pepper for heat.
4. In a salad bowl, combine the seaweed, cucumber, and dressing. Toss thoroughly.
5. Sprinkle the toasted sesame seeds on top before serving.

NUTRITIONAL VALUE (PER 100 G): 80 kcal, 3 g protein, 3 g fat, 10 g carbohydrates, 2 g fiber

DECORATION TIP: Garnish with thin lime slices or a few fresh cilantro leaves for added aroma.

BEETROOT DELIGHT – ROASTED BEET SALAD WITH WALNUTS

DESCRIPTION: This hearty and flavorful salad combines the rich taste of roasted beets, the nutty texture of walnuts, and the creaminess of a lemon dressing. A perfect choice for a cozy lunch or dinner.
INGREDIENTS:
- 2 medium beets (about 300 g), roasted and cut into cubes
- 1/4 cup (30 g) toasted walnuts
- 3 1/2 oz (100 g) salad greens (arugula or spinach)
- 1/4 cup (60 ml) natural yogurt
- 1 tbsp (15 ml) lemon juice
- 1 tsp (5 ml) honey
- A pinch of salt and freshly ground pepper

COOKING TIME: Preparation: 10 minutes, Cooking: 40 minutes (for roasting the beets)
INSTRUCTIONS:
1. Preheat the oven to 200°C (390°F). Wrap the beets in foil and roast for 35–40 minutes until tender. Cool, peel, and cut into cubes.
2. Lightly toast the walnuts in a dry skillet until golden.
3. Wash and dry the salad greens.
4. In a small bowl, mix the natural yogurt, lemon juice, honey, salt, and pepper for the dressing.
5. In a salad bowl, combine the roasted beets, salad greens, and walnuts. Drizzle with the dressing and gently toss.
6. Serve the salad immediately, enjoying its harmony of textures and flavors.

NUTRITIONAL VALUE (PER 100 G): 120 kcal, 4 g protein, 5 g fat, 14 g carbohydrates, 3 g fiber
DECORATION TIP: Garnish the salad with a few drops of yogurt or thin slices of lemon for a bright accent.

POMEGRANATE FRESHNESS – QUINOA, SPINACH, AND POMEGRANATE SALAD

DESCRIPTION: This vibrant and refreshing salad combines the delicate texture of quinoa, the rich flavor of spinach, and the sweetness of pomegranate seeds. A light lemon dressing enhances the natural flavors, making it a perfect choice for lunch or dinner.
INGREDIENTS:
- 1/2 cup (90 g) cooked quinoa
- 3 1/2 oz (100 g) fresh spinach
- 1/2 cup (75 g) pomegranate seeds
- 1/4 cup (30 g) toasted pumpkin seeds
- 2 tbsp (30 ml) olive oil
- 1 tbsp (15 ml) lemon juice
- 1 tsp (5 ml) honey
- A pinch of salt and freshly ground pepper

COOKING TIME: Preparation: 10 minutes
INSTRUCTIONS:
1. Cook the quinoa according to the package instructions and cool.
2. Wash the spinach and pat dry.
3. Lightly toast the pumpkin seeds in a dry skillet until golden.
4. In a small bowl, mix olive oil, lemon juice, honey, salt, and pepper to make the dressing.
5. In a salad bowl, combine quinoa, spinach, pomegranate seeds, and toasted pumpkin seeds. Drizzle with the dressing and gently toss.
6. Serve the salad immediately, enjoying its freshness and rich flavors.

NUTRITIONAL VALUE (PER 100 G): 130 kcal, 4 g protein, 6 g fat, 14 g carbohydrates, 3 g fiber
DECORATION TIP: Garnish the salad with a few pomegranate seeds and fresh mint leaves for a bright accent.

EASTERN CHARM – EGGPLANT AND TAHINI SALAD

DESCRIPTION: This hearty and aromatic salad combines the tenderness of roasted eggplant with the rich flavor of tahini. The light Eastern touch makes it a perfect choice for lunch or dinner.
INGREDIENTS:

- 1 medium eggplant (about 300 g), cut into cubes
- 3 1/2 oz (100 g) salad greens (arugula, spinach, or a mix)
- 1/4 cup (30 g) toasted pine nuts
- 2 tbsp (30 ml) tahini
- 1 tbsp (15 ml) lemon juice
- 1 tsp (5 ml) honey (or agave syrup for vegans)
- 1 tbsp (15 ml) olive oil
- A pinch of salt and freshly ground pepper

COOKING TIME: Preparation: 10 minutes, Cooking: 20 minutes
INSTRUCTIONS:
1. Preheat the oven to 200°C (390°F).
2. Place the cubed eggplant on a baking sheet, drizzle with olive oil, sprinkle with salt and pepper, and toss. Roast for 20 minutes until soft and lightly golden.
3. Lightly toast the pine nuts in a dry skillet until golden.
4. Wash and dry the salad greens.
5. In a small bowl, mix tahini, lemon juice, honey, salt, and pepper. If the sauce is too thick, add a little water to reach the desired consistency.
6. In a salad bowl, combine the salad greens, roasted eggplant, and toasted pine nuts. Drizzle with the tahini dressing and gently toss.
7. Serve the salad immediately, enjoying its rich flavor and aroma.

NUTRITIONAL VALUE (PER 100 G): 140 kcal, 3 g protein, 8 g fat, 12 g carbohydrates, 4 g fiber
DECORATION TIP: Garnish the salad with an additional spoonful of tahini or sprinkle finely chopped fresh cilantro for a bright Eastern accent.

SPICY PUMPKIN – CHICKPEA AND CORIANDER SALAD

DESCRIPTION: This hearty and aromatic salad combines the sweetness of roasted pumpkin, the tenderness of chickpeas, and the brightness of coriander.
INGREDIENTS:

- 1 cup (150 g) cubed pumpkin
- 1/2 cup (90 g) cooked or canned chickpeas, rinsed and drained
- 3 1/2 oz (100 g) salad greens (arugula, spinach, or mix)
- 1/4 cup (15 g) fresh coriander, finely chopped
- 1/4 tsp ground cumin
- 1/4 tsp ground paprika
- 2 tbsp (30 ml) olive oil
- 1 tbsp (15 ml) lemon juice
- 1 tsp (5 ml) honey (or agave syrup for vegans)
- A pinch of salt and freshly ground pepper

COOKING TIME: Preparation: 10 minutes, Cooking: 25 minutes
INSTRUCTIONS:
1. Preheat the oven to 200°C (390°F).
2. Place the pumpkin cubes on a baking sheet, drizzle with 1 tablespoon of olive oil, and sprinkle with cumin, paprika, salt, and pepper. Roast for 20–25 minutes until soft and lightly golden.
3. Wash and dry the salad greens.
4. In a small bowl, mix the remaining olive oil, lemon juice, honey, salt, and pepper for the dressing.
5. In a salad bowl, combine the roasted pumpkin, chickpeas, salad greens, and chopped coriander. Drizzle with the dressing and gently toss.
6. Serve the salad warm or chilled, enjoying its rich flavor.

NUTRITIONAL VALUE (PER 100 G): 130 kcal, 4 g protein, 6 g fat, 15 g carbohydrates, 3 g fiber
DECORATION TIP: Garnish the salad with a few fresh coriander leaves or sprinkle with crushed pumpkin seeds for extra texture.

GREEN FRESHNESS – CUCUMBER, AVOCADO, AND GREEN ONION SALAD

DESCRIPTION: This light and refreshing salad combines the crunch of cucumber, the tenderness of avocado, and the sharpness of green onions. The light lemon dressing enhances the natural flavors, making it perfect for lunch or dinner.
INGREDIENTS:
- 1 large cucumber, sliced into half-moons
- 1 ripe avocado, diced
- 2 stalks of green onion, finely chopped
- 3 1/2 oz (100 g) salad greens (arugula, spinach, or mix)
- 2 tbsp (30 ml) olive oil
- 1 tbsp (15 ml) lemon juice
- A pinch of salt and freshly ground pepper

COOKING TIME: Preparation: 10 minutes
INSTRUCTIONS:
1. Slice the cucumber into half-moons and dice the avocado.
2. Wash and dry the salad greens.
3. Finely chop the green onions.
4. In a small bowl, mix the olive oil, lemon juice, salt, and pepper for the dressing.
5. In a salad bowl, combine the salad greens, cucumber, avocado, and green onion. Drizzle with the dressing and gently toss.
6. Serve the salad immediately, enjoying its freshness.

NUTRITIONAL VALUE (PER 100 G): 120 kcal, 2 g protein, 8 g fat, 9 g carbohydrates, 3 g fiber
DECORATION TIP: Garnish the salad with thin lemon slices or sprinkle with a pinch of black sesame seeds for extra texture and color.

WARM CHICKPEA – CHICKPEA, SPINACH, AND ROASTED VEGETABLE SALAD

DESCRIPTION: This hearty and aromatic salad combines warm chickpeas, tender spinach, and the sweet flavor of roasted vegetables. A perfect dish for a cozy lunch or dinner.
INGREDIENTS:
- 1 cup (150 g) cooked or canned chickpeas, rinsed and drained
- 1 medium bell pepper, sliced into strips
- 1 small zucchini, sliced into rounds
- 1/2 red onion, sliced into wedges
- 3 1/2 oz (100 g) fresh spinach
- 2 tbsp (30 ml) olive oil
- 1 tbsp (15 ml) lemon juice
- 1 tsp (5 ml) honey (or agave syrup for vegans)
- A pinch of salt and freshly ground pepper
- 1/4 tsp ground paprika

COOKING TIME: Preparation: 10 minutes, cooking: 15 minutes
INSTRUCTIONS:
1. Heat 1 tablespoon of olive oil in a skillet over medium heat.
2. Add the bell pepper strips, zucchini, and red onion. Cook for 10–12 minutes until the vegetables are tender and slightly browned. Sprinkle with paprika, salt, and pepper, and stir.
3. In a separate skillet, heat the remaining oil and lightly sauté the chickpeas for 3–5 minutes until warm.
4. Rinse and dry the spinach.
5. In a small bowl, mix lemon juice, honey, salt, and pepper for the dressing.
6. In a salad bowl, combine the warm chickpeas, roasted vegetables, and spinach. Drizzle with the dressing and toss gently.
7. Serve immediately, enjoying the warm aromas.

NUTRITIONAL VALUE (PER 100 G): 130 kcal, 4 g protein, 6 g fat, 14 g carbohydrates, 3 g fiber
DECORATION TIP: Garnish the salad with crushed nuts (walnuts or almonds) or sprinkle with fresh parsley for a vibrant touch.

LIGHT SALADS FOR EVERY DAY: FRESHNESS AND EASE IN ANY SEASON

Light salads embody simplicity, freshness, and harmony with nature. This section brings together recipes that are perfect for a quick and healthy lunch or dinner. These salads are designed for moments when you crave something tasty and nourishing, but without the heaviness. Each recipe is crafted with the goal of supporting your health while enjoying the abundance of seasonal produce that provides the body with energy and lightness.

Light salads are an art of combining fresh, crunchy vegetables, vibrant fruits, and fragrant herbs. We have carefully created dishes that are easy to adapt to various tastes and preferences, and can be made from accessible ingredients. You'll find a variety of combinations here: from refreshing cucumbers and juicy tomatoes to the exotic notes of mango or citrus fruits. All of these ingredients are packed with vitamins and antioxidants that help maintain vitality and strengthen the immune system.

This section includes not only classic vegetable combinations but also innovative recipes with added grains, nuts, and seeds. For example, a light salad with quinoa, fresh cucumbers, and a lemon dressing is a true source of plant-based protein that keeps you feeling full without overwhelming your system. A salad with strawberries and spinach, dressed with balsamic vinegar, creates a delightful balance of sweet and tangy notes, adding lightness and brightness to your menu.

Dressing plays a key role in balancing the flavors of light salads. In this section, you'll find recipes for simple yet incredibly tasty dressings that enhance the flavor of each ingredient and give the dish a unique character. A lemon-honey dressing adds freshness and tanginess, while olive oil with a dash of apple cider vinegar brings lightness and a subtle aroma. Each dressing is designed to maintain the natural taste of the ingredients and ensure a harmonious combination.

Light salads are not just food; they are a way of life that helps maintain harmony with nature and your body. At any time of year, these salads will delight you with freshness and natural aromas. Whether it's spring, when you crave something refreshing, or winter, when a light salad helps balance a heartier menu — these recipes will always be relevant. Let light salads become your favorite dish that brings joy and a sense of ease every day!

SUMMER REFRESHMENT — CUCUMBER, DILL, AND LEMON JUICE SALAD

DESCRIPTION: This refreshing and light salad combines crunchy cucumber, aromatic dill, and a tangy lemon juice. An ideal choice for a hot summer day or as a side dish.

INGREDIENTS:
- 2 large cucumbers, sliced into thin rounds
- 2 tablespoons (15 g) fresh dill, finely chopped
- 1 tablespoon (15 ml) lemon juice
- 1 tablespoon (15 ml) olive oil
- Pinch of salt and freshly ground black pepper

COOKING TIME: preparation: 10 minutes

INSTRUCTIONS:
1. Slice the cucumbers into thin rounds or half-moons if the cucumbers are large.
2. Finely chop the dill.
3. In a small bowl, combine lemon juice, olive oil, salt, and pepper for the dressing.
4. In a salad bowl, combine the cucumbers and dill. Pour the dressing over and toss well.
5. Serve the salad immediately or chill for 10 minutes for a more refreshing taste.

NUTRITIONAL VALUE (PER 100 G): 40 kcal, 1 g protein, 3 g fat, 3 g carbohydrates, 1 g fiber

DECORATION TIP: Garnish the salad with extra sprigs of dill or thin slices of lemon for a bright accent.

TOMATO DELIGHT — LIGHT TOMATO AND BASIL SALAD

DESCRIPTION: This simple and aromatic salad combines the sweetness of fresh tomatoes, the richness of basil, and the lightness of olive oil. A classic dish, perfect for a light lunch or dinner.

INGREDIENTS:
- 2 large tomatoes, sliced into wedges
- 1/2 cup (75 g) cherry tomatoes, halved
- 1/4 cup (15 g) fresh basil leaves
- 2 tablespoons (30 ml) olive oil
- 1 tablespoon (15 ml) balsamic vinegar
- Pinch of salt and freshly ground black pepper

COOKING TIME: preparation: 10 minutes

INSTRUCTIONS:
1. Slice the large tomatoes into wedges and halve the cherry tomatoes.
2. Arrange the tomatoes on a serving plate, alternating the wedges and halved cherry tomatoes.
3. Place the basil leaves on top of the tomatoes.
4. In a small bowl, combine the olive oil, balsamic vinegar, salt, and pepper for the dressing.
5. Drizzle the dressing over the salad just before serving.
6. Serve the salad immediately, enjoying its freshness and simplicity.

NUTRITIONAL VALUE (PER 100 G): 60 kcal, 1 g protein, 4 g fat, 5 g carbohydrates, 1 g fiber

DECORATION TIP: Garnish the salad with a few drops of balsamic glaze or sprinkle with coarse sea salt for an extra touch.

CRUNCHY FRESHNESS — YOUNG CABBAGE SALAD WITH APPLE

DESCRIPTION: This light and refreshing salad combines crispy young cabbage, juicy apple, and a tangy lemon-yogurt dressing. A perfect choice for lunch or as a side dish.

INGREDIENTS:
- 2 cups (150 g) finely chopped young cabbage
- 1 large green apple, grated or sliced into thin strips
- 1 tablespoon (15 g) finely chopped dill
- 2 tablespoons (30 ml) natural yogurt
- 1 tablespoon (15 ml) lemon juice
- 1 teaspoon (5 ml) honey (or agave syrup for vegans)
- Pinch of salt and freshly ground black pepper

COOKING TIME: preparation: 10 minutes

INSTRUCTIONS:
1. Finely slice the young cabbage, grate the apple, or slice it into thin strips.
2. In a small bowl, combine yogurt, lemon juice, honey, salt, and pepper for the dressing.
3. In a salad bowl, mix the cabbage, apple, and dill. Drizzle with the dressing and toss well.
4. Let the salad sit for 5–10 minutes before serving, allowing the cabbage to soften and absorb the dressing.

NUTRITIONAL VALUE (PER 100 G): 50 kcal, 1 g protein, 1 g fat, 10 g carbohydrates, 2 g fiber

DECORATION TIP: Garnish the salad with thin apple slices or sprinkle with crushed nuts for extra crunch.

SWEET CRUNCH — CARROT SALAD WITH RAISINS AND NUTS

DESCRIPTION: This vibrant and sweet salad combines the tenderness of carrots, the juiciness of raisins, and the crunch of nuts. A light honey dressing enhances the flavor, making it perfect for lunch or a snack.

INGREDIENTS:
- 2 medium carrots (about 200 g), grated coarsely
- 1/4 cup (40 g) raisins
- 1/4 cup (30 g) roasted walnuts or almonds, coarsely chopped
- 2 tablespoons (30 ml) natural yogurt
- 1 tablespoon (15 ml) lemon juice
- 1 teaspoon (5 ml) honey (or agave syrup for vegans)
- Pinch of salt

COOKING TIME: preparation: 10 minutes

INSTRUCTIONS:
1. Grate the carrots coarsely.
2. Soak the raisins in warm water for 5 minutes, then dry them.
3. Lightly toast the nuts in a dry pan until golden brown.
4. In a small bowl, mix yogurt, lemon juice, honey, and a pinch of salt for the dressing.
5. In a salad bowl, combine the carrots, raisins, and nuts. Drizzle with the dressing and toss thoroughly.
6. Serve immediately or let the salad sit for 5–10 minutes for a more intense flavor.

NUTRITIONAL VALUE (PER 100 G): 120 kcal, 2 g protein, 6 g fat, 14 g carbohydrates, 2 g fiber

DECORATION TIP: Garnish the salad with whole nuts or small mint leaves for extra freshness.

SPRING LIGHTNESS — RADISH SALAD WITH SOUR CREAM AND GREEN ONION

DESCRIPTION: This fresh and light salad combines crunchy radishes, aromatic green onions, and delicate sour cream. A simple and delicious dish, perfect for a spring lunch or dinner.

INGREDIENTS:
- 1 bunch of radishes (about 150 g), sliced thinly
- 2 stalks of green onion, finely chopped
- 3 1/2 oz (100 g) sour cream (10–15% fat)
- 1 tablespoon (15 ml) lemon juice
- Pinch of salt and freshly ground black pepper

COOKING TIME: preparation: 10 minutes

INSTRUCTIONS:
1. Slice the radishes thinly.
2. Finely chop the green onions.
3. In a small bowl, mix sour cream, lemon juice, salt, and pepper for the dressing.
4. In a salad bowl, combine the radishes and green onions. Drizzle with the dressing and toss thoroughly.
5. Serve the salad immediately, enjoying its freshness and delicate flavor.

NUTRITIONAL VALUE (PER 100 G): 80 kcal, 2 g protein, 6 g fat, 5 g carbohydrates, 1 g fiber

DECORATION TIP: Garnish the salad with thin radish slices or small sprigs of dill for extra appeal.

CITRUS INSPIRATION — FRESH SPINACH SALAD WITH EGG AND LEMON DRESSING

DESCRIPTION: This light and nutritious salad combines tender spinach, boiled egg, and a refreshing lemon dressing. A perfect choice for a healthy lunch or dinner.

INGREDIENTS:
- 3 1/2 oz (100 g) fresh spinach
- 2 boiled eggs, sliced
- 1/4 cup (30 g) roasted pumpkin seeds
- 2 tablespoons (30 ml) olive oil
- 1 tablespoon (15 ml) lemon juice
- 1 teaspoon (5 ml) honey
- Pinch of salt and freshly ground black pepper

COOKING TIME: preparation: 10 minutes

INSTRUCTIONS:
1. Wash and dry the spinach.
2. Slice the boiled eggs.
3. Lightly roast the pumpkin seeds in a dry pan until golden brown.
4. In a small bowl, mix olive oil, lemon juice, honey, salt, and pepper for the dressing.
5. In a salad bowl, combine the spinach, eggs, and pumpkin seeds. Drizzle with the dressing and toss gently.
6. Serve the salad immediately, enjoying its freshness and harmonious flavors.

NUTRITIONAL VALUE (PER 100 G): 130 kcal, 5 g protein, 9 g fat, 5 g carbohydrates, 2 g fiber

DECORATION TIP: Garnish the salad with lemon slices or sprinkle with finely chopped parsley for an extra touch.

SUMMER CRUNCH — GREEN BEAN AND CHERRY TOMATO SALAD

DESCRIPTION: This light and refreshing salad combines crunchy green beans, juicy cherry tomatoes, and a tangy lemon-olive oil dressing. A perfect choice for a summer lunch or dinner.

INGREDIENTS:
- 1 cup (150 g) green beans, cooked to a crisp texture
- 1/2 cup (75 g) cherry tomatoes, halved
- 3 1/2 oz (100 g) salad greens (arugula, spinach, or a mix)
- 2 tablespoons (30 ml) olive oil
- 1 tablespoon (15 ml) lemon juice
- 1 teaspoon (5 ml) Dijon mustard
- Pinch of salt and freshly ground black pepper

COOKING TIME: preparation: 10 minutes

INSTRUCTIONS:
1. Cook the green beans in salted water for 3–4 minutes to a crisp texture, then rinse under cold water and pat dry.
2. Halve the cherry tomatoes.
3. Wash and dry the salad greens.
4. In a small bowl, mix olive oil, lemon juice, Dijon mustard, salt, and pepper for the dressing.
5. In a salad bowl, combine the green beans, cherry tomatoes, and salad greens. Drizzle with the dressing and toss gently.
6. Serve the salad immediately, enjoying its freshness and flavor.

NUTRITIONAL VALUE (PER 100 G): 90 kcal, 2 g protein, 6 g fat, 7 g carbohydrates, 2 g fiber

DECORATION TIP: Garnish the salad with a few lemon slices or a pinch of ground black pepper for an extra touch.

ITALIAN SIMPLICITY — ARUGULA, PARMESAN, AND LEMON DRESSING SALAD

DESCRIPTION: This light and elegant salad combines the spiciness of arugula, the tenderness of parmesan, and the freshness of lemon dressing. A perfect choice for a quick lunch or as a side dish to main courses.

INGREDIENTS:
- 3 1/2 oz (100 g) fresh arugula
- 1/4 cup (30 g) thinly sliced parmesan
- 2 tablespoons (30 ml) olive oil
- 1 tablespoon (15 ml) lemon juice
- Pinch of salt and freshly ground black pepper

COOKING TIME: preparation: 5 minutes

INSTRUCTIONS:
1. Wash the arugula under cold water and pat dry.
2. In a small bowl, mix olive oil, lemon juice, salt, and pepper for the dressing.
3. In a salad bowl, combine the arugula and thinly sliced parmesan.
4. Drizzle with the dressing and toss gently.
5. Serve immediately, enjoying the fresh taste and delicate texture.

NUTRITIONAL VALUE (PER 100 G): 120 kcal, 4 g protein, 9 g fat, 3 g carbohydrates, 1 g fiber

DECORATION TIP: Garnish the salad with a few drops of balsamic vinegar or sprinkle with ground black pepper for an added touch of sophistication.

REFRESHING SIMPLICITY — CABBAGE, CARROT, AND APPLE CIDER VINEGAR SALAD

DESCRIPTION: This crunchy and refreshing salad combines finely shredded cabbage, the sweetness of carrots, and the tanginess of apple cider vinegar. A great choice for a light side dish or a healthy snack.

INGREDIENTS:
- 2 cups (150 g) finely shredded white cabbage
- 1 medium carrot (about 100 g), grated
- 2 tablespoons (30 ml) apple cider vinegar
- 1 tablespoon (15 ml) olive oil
- 1 teaspoon (5 ml) honey (or agave syrup for vegans)
- Pinch of salt and freshly ground black pepper

COOKING TIME: preparation: 10 minutes

INSTRUCTIONS:
1. Finely shred the cabbage and grate the carrot.
2. In a small bowl, mix the apple cider vinegar, olive oil, honey, salt, and pepper for the dressing.
3. In a salad bowl, combine the cabbage and carrot.
4. Drizzle with the dressing and toss thoroughly.
5. Let the salad sit for 5-10 minutes for a more intense flavor, then serve.

NUTRITIONAL VALUE (PER 100 G): 60 kcal, 1 g protein, 3 g fat, 8 g carbohydrates, 2 g fiber

DECORATION TIP: Garnish the salad with fresh parsley leaves or sprinkle with sesame seeds for added texture.

MEDITERRANEAN BREEZE — CUCUMBER, MINT, AND FETA SALAD

DESCRIPTION: This light and aromatic salad combines crispy cucumbers, fresh mint, and salty feta. The refreshing taste is perfect for a summer lunch or dinner.

INGREDIENTS:
- 2 large cucumbers, sliced into half-circles
- 1/4 cup (40 g) feta, crumbled
- 2 tablespoons (15 g) fresh mint, finely chopped
- 2 tablespoons (30 ml) olive oil
- 1 tablespoon (15 ml) lemon juice
- Pinch of salt and freshly ground black pepper

COOKING TIME: preparation: 10 minutes

INSTRUCTIONS:
1. Slice the cucumbers into half-circles.
2. Finely chop the fresh mint.
3. In a small bowl, mix the olive oil, lemon juice, salt, and pepper for the dressing.
4. In a salad bowl, combine the cucumbers, mint, and crumbled feta. Drizzle with the dressing and gently toss.
5. Serve the salad immediately, enjoying its freshness and vibrant flavor.

NUTRITIONAL VALUE (PER 100 G): 80 kcal, 2 g protein, 6 g fat, 4 g carbohydrates, 1 g fiber

DECORATION TIP: Garnish the salad with fresh mint leaves or add a few thin slices of lemon for a bright accent.

SUMMER INSPIRATION — ZUCCHINI SALAD WITH LEMON OIL

DESCRIPTION: This light and aromatic fresh zucchini salad with lemon oil is the perfect refreshment on hot summer days. A simple yet elegant dish that will elevate any lunch or dinner.

INGREDIENTS:
- 2 small zucchinis, sliced into thin ribbons or rounds
- 2 tablespoons (30 ml) lemon oil (or olive oil with lemon juice)
- 1 tablespoon (15 ml) lemon juice
- 1 teaspoon (5 ml) honey (or agave syrup for vegans)
- Pinch of salt and freshly ground black pepper
- 1/4 cup (30 g) toasted almond flakes or pine nuts
- A few fresh mint or basil leaves for decoration

COOKING TIME: preparation: 10 minutes

INSTRUCTIONS:
1. Slice the zucchinis into thin ribbons using a vegetable peeler or into rounds.
2. In a small bowl, mix the lemon oil, lemon juice, honey, salt, and pepper for the dressing.
3. Place the zucchini in a salad bowl, drizzle with the dressing, and gently toss.
4. Before serving, sprinkle the salad with toasted almond flakes or pine nuts.
5. Garnish with fresh mint or basil leaves for extra freshness and aroma.

NUTRITIONAL VALUE (PER 100 G): 70 kcal, 2 g protein, 5 g fat, 4 g carbohydrates, 1 g fiber

DECORATION TIP: For a bright accent, add a few thin slices of lemon or sprinkle with finely grated lemon zest.

LIGHT SPRING MIX — SALAD WITH GREEN PEAS, RADISH, AND MINT DRESSING

DESCRIPTION: This bright and refreshing salad combines the sweetness of green peas, the crunch of radish, and the refreshing taste of mint dressing. An ideal choice for a spring lunch or dinner.

INGREDIENTS:
- 1 cup (150 g) fresh or frozen green peas
- 1 bunch of radishes (about 150 g), sliced thinly
- 3 1/2 ounces (100 g) salad greens (arugula, spinach, or mix)
- 2 tablespoons (30 ml) olive oil
- 1 tablespoon (15 ml) lemon juice
- 1 teaspoon (5 ml) honey (or agave syrup for vegans)
- 1 tablespoon (15 g) finely chopped fresh mint
- Pinch of salt and freshly ground black pepper

COOKING TIME: preparation: 10 minutes

INSTRUCTIONS:
1. If using frozen peas, pour boiling water over them for 2 minutes, then drain and rinse with cold water. Fresh peas can be used immediately.
2. Slice the radishes into thin rounds.
3. Wash and dry the salad greens.
4. In a small bowl, mix olive oil, lemon juice, honey, chopped mint, salt, and pepper for the dressing.
5. In a salad bowl, combine peas, radishes, and salad greens. Drizzle with the dressing and gently toss.
6. Serve the salad immediately, enjoying its freshness and spring aromas.

NUTRITIONAL VALUE (PER 100 G): 90 kcal, 2 g protein, 5 g fat, 8 g carbohydrates, 2 g fiber

DECORATION TIP: Garnish the salad with a few whole mint leaves or lemon slices for extra freshness.

ELIXIRS OF FLAVOR: THE MAGIC OF SALAD DRESSINGS

A **DRESSING** is not just an addition—it is a **magical key** that unlocks the full potential of every ingredient. It can **enhance the freshness of greens, deepen the warmth of spices, soften sharp flavors, or bring a dish into perfect harmony**. In this section, we have gathered **unique elixirs of flavor** that not only make salads unforgettable but also **infuse them with the power of health**.

Health in Every Drop

A delicious dressing can be **not only aromatic and balanced but also incredibly beneficial**. Every drop is a **treasure trove of nutrients** that support **digestion, energy, metabolism, and immunity**.

✓ **Healthy fats** (*olive, flaxseed, avocado, and nut oils*) — nourish cells, help absorb vitamins A, D, E, and K, and support heart and vascular health.
✓ **Acids** (*lemon, lime, pomegranate juice, natural vinegars*) — stimulate metabolism, aid digestion, and enhance iron absorption from vegetables.
✓ **Antioxidants and phytonutrients** (*herbs, spices, garlic, turmeric, ginger*) — neutralize free radicals and slow down the aging process.
✓ **Prebiotics and enzymes** (*yogurt, kefir, miso, tahini*) — support gut microbiota and promote comfortable digestion.
✓ **Natural sweetness** (*honey, maple syrup, date paste*) — adds a delicate caramel note without causing blood sugar spikes.

Flavor Transformation: The Alchemy of Dressings

A **DRESSING** is a **delicate art of balance**, where every note plays a crucial role:

◆ **Refreshes** (*citrus, yogurt, mint, basil*) – perfect for light summer salads.
◆ **Adds spice** (*mustard, garlic, chili, coriander*) – brings out a bold, zesty flavor.
◆ **Creates richness** (*nut butters, tahini, yogurt, avocado*) – makes a dish more satisfying.
◆ **Softens and rounds out flavors** (*olive oil, honey, balsamic vinegar*) – brings harmony to the dish.

A **DRESSING is pure magic**, where just a few drops can completely transform the mood of a salad. **Embrace the art of experimentation**, add your own signature touches, and explore new dimensions of flavor!

GOLDEN VINAIGRETTE

DESCRIPTION: A classic French-style vinaigrette with a perfect balance of acidity and mild sweetness. This dressing is ideal for green salads, roasted vegetables, and grain bowls, adding a bright and refreshing touch.

BENEFITS: **Rich in Omega-9 fatty acids and antioxidants.**
- **Olive oil** – protects blood vessels and reduces inflammation.
- **Dijon mustard** – boosts metabolism and adds a tangy kick.
- **Apple cider vinegar** – supports digestion and balances pH levels.

INGREDIENTS:
- 2 tbsp (30 ml) olive oil
- 1 tbsp (15 ml) apple cider vinegar
- 1 tsp (5 ml) Dijon mustard
- 1 tsp (5 ml) honey (or agave syrup)
- A pinch of salt and freshly ground black pepper

COOKING TIME: 5 minutes

INSTRUCTIONS:
1. Combine all ingredients in a small bowl or a glass jar.
2. Whisk or shake well until fully blended.
3. Let sit for 5 minutes to allow the flavors to meld before using.

NUTRITIONAL VALUE (PER 100 G): 120 kcal, 0.3 g protein, 12 g fat, 3 g carbohydrates, 0 g fiber
NUTRITIONAL VALUE PER SERVING: 60 kcal, 0.15 g protein, 6 g fat, 1.5 g carbohydrates, 0 g fiber
SERVING TIP: For a more aromatic touch, add a pinch of dried herbs de Provence or a bit of freshly grated lemon zest.

MEDITERRANEAN LEMON BASIL DRESSING

DESCRIPTION: A vibrant and refreshing Mediterranean-style dressing with the zesty brightness of lemon and the aromatic depth of fresh basil. This dressing pairs perfectly with leafy greens, grilled vegetables, and Mediterranean-inspired grain bowls.

BENEFITS: Rich in vitamins C and K, improves circulation.
- **Lemon** – a great source of vitamin C and a natural detoxifier.
- **Basil** – a powerful antioxidant that slows down aging.
- **Garlic** – strengthens the immune system.

INGREDIENTS:
- 3 tbsp (45 ml) olive oil
- 1 tbsp (15 ml) lemon juice
- 1 tsp (5 ml) lemon zest
- 2 tbsp (10 g) finely chopped fresh basil
- 1 garlic clove, minced
- A pinch of salt and freshly ground black pepper

COOKING TIME: 5 minutes

INSTRUCTIONS:
1. In a small bowl or a glass jar, combine all ingredients.
2. Whisk or shake well until fully blended.
3. Let the dressing sit for 5 minutes to allow the flavors to meld before using.

NUTRITIONAL VALUE (PER 100 G): 110 kcal, 0.2 g protein, 11 g fat, 1 g carbohydrates, 0.3 g fiber
NUTRITIONAL VALUE PER SERVING: 55 kcal, 0.1 g protein, 5.5 g fat, 0.5 g carbohydrates, 0.15 g fiber
SERVING TIP: For an extra Mediterranean touch, add a pinch of dried oregano or a few drops of balsamic vinegar to enhance the depth of flavor.

GARLIC LEMON YOGURT DRESSING

DESCRIPTION: A creamy and tangy dressing with the refreshing zest of lemon and the bold aroma of garlic. This dressing is perfect for Mediterranean salads, grain bowls, and roasted vegetables, adding a smooth yet zesty flavor.
BENEFITS: Supports gut microbiota, rich in probiotics.
- **Plain yogurt** – a source of beneficial bacteria.
- **Lemon** – refreshes and aids fat digestion.
- **Dill** – promotes detoxification.

INGREDIENTS:
- ½ cup (120 g) plain yogurt
- 1 tbsp (15 ml) lemon juice
- 1 tsp (5 ml) olive oil
- 1 garlic clove, grated
- A pinch of salt
- 1 tbsp (5 g) finely chopped fresh dill (optional)

COOKING TIME: 5 minutes
INSTRUCTIONS:
1. In a small bowl, whisk together the yogurt, lemon juice, olive oil, and grated garlic.
2. Add salt and mix until smooth.
3. If using, stir in finely chopped dill for extra freshness.
4. Chill for a few minutes before serving to enhance the flavors.

NUTRITIONAL VALUE (PER 100 G): 60 kcal, 3.5 g protein, 3 g fat, 4 g carbohydrates, 0.2 g fiber
NUTRITIONAL VALUE PER SERVING: 30 kcal, 1.75 g protein, 1.5 g fat, 2 g carbohydrates, 0.1 g fiber
SERVING TIP: For a silkier texture, blend the dressing for a few seconds. Add a pinch of ground cumin or black pepper for a subtle depth of flavor.

.

ASIAN SESAME GINGER DRESSING

DESCRIPTION: A flavorful and aromatic Asian-inspired dressing with the nutty richness of sesame, the umami depth of soy sauce, and the warmth of fresh ginger. Perfect for crunchy cabbage salads, noodle bowls, or as a marinade for grilled vegetables.
BENEFITS: Supports brain function, rich in magnesium and antioxidants.
- **Sesame oil** – promotes skin and joint health.
- **Ginger** – stimulates circulation and provides warmth.
- **Soy sauce** – a source of essential amino acids.

INGREDIENTS:
- 2 tbsp (30 ml) soy sauce
- 1 tbsp (15 ml) sesame oil
- 1 tbsp (15 ml) apple cider vinegar
- 1 tsp (5 ml) honey (or maple syrup)
- 1 tsp (5 g) grated fresh ginger
- 1 tsp (5 g) sesame seeds

COOKING TIME: 5 minutes
INSTRUCTIONS:
1. In a small bowl or jar, whisk together the soy sauce, sesame oil, vinegar, honey, and grated ginger.
2. Stir in sesame seeds for extra texture and nuttiness.
3. Let the dressing sit for 5 minutes before serving to allow the flavors to meld.

NUTRITIONAL VALUE (PER 100 G): 80 kcal, 2 g protein, 6 g fat, 5 g carbohydrates, 0.5 g fiber
NUTRITIONAL VALUE PER SERVING: 40 kcal, 1 g protein, 3 g fat, 2.5 g carbohydrates, 0.25 g fiber
SERVING TIP: For a spicier kick, add a pinch of red pepper flakes or a dash of Sriracha. To enhance the depth of flavor, lightly toast the sesame seeds before adding them to the dressing.

CREAMY AVOCADO LIME DRESSING

DESCRIPTION:
A rich and velvety dressing with the creaminess of avocado and the refreshing zest of lime. This dressing pairs perfectly with taco salads, grain bowls, and roasted vegetables, adding a smooth and citrusy touch.
BENEFITS: A source of healthy fats and fiber, nourishes the skin.
- **Avocado** – rich in potassium, helps maintain fluid balance.
- **Lime** – refreshes and supports body detoxification.
- **Greek yogurt** – strengthens gut microbiota.

INGREDIENTS:
- ½ ripe avocado
- 2 tbsp (30 g) Greek yogurt
- 1 tbsp (15 ml) lime juice
- 1 tbsp (15 ml) olive oil
- A pinch of salt

COOKING TIME: 5 minutes
INSTRUCTIONS:
1. In a blender or food processor, combine avocado, Greek yogurt, lime juice, olive oil, and salt.
2. Blend until smooth and creamy. If needed, add a splash of water to adjust consistency.
3. Use immediately or refrigerate for up to 2 days.

NUTRITIONAL VALUE (PER 100 G): 90 kcal, 2 g protein, 8 g fat, 4 g carbohydrates, 2 g fiber
NUTRITIONAL VALUE PER SERVING: 45 kcal, 1 g protein, 4 g fat, 2 g carbohydrates, 1 g fiber
SERVING TIP:
For extra zest, add a pinch of lime zest or a few fresh cilantro leaves before blending. If you prefer a thinner consistency, mix in a tablespoon of water or buttermilk.

NUTTY MAPLE DRESSING

DESCRIPTION:
A smooth and slightly sweet dressing with the richness of nut butter and the natural caramel notes of maple syrup. This dressing is perfect for autumn salads, roasted root vegetables, and grain bowls, adding a nutty depth and a touch of sweetness.
BENEFITS: Supports hormonal balance, rich in magnesium.
- **Almond butter** – improves skin and hair health.
- **Maple syrup** – a natural source of antioxidants.
- **Cinnamon** – helps regulate blood sugar levels.

INGREDIENTS:
- 2 tbsp (30 ml) maple syrup
- 2 tbsp (30 g) almond butter (or peanut butter)
- 1 tbsp (15 ml) apple cider vinegar
- A pinch of cinnamon
- A pinch of salt

COOKING TIME: 5 minutes
INSTRUCTIONS:
1. In a small bowl, whisk together the maple syrup and almond butter until smooth.
2. Add apple cider vinegar, cinnamon, and salt, whisking until fully combined.
3. If the dressing is too thick, add a teaspoon of water to reach the desired consistency.

NUTRITIONAL VALUE (PER 100 G): 120 kcal, 2 g protein, 6 g fat, 14 g carbohydrates, 1 g fiber
NUTRITIONAL VALUE PER SERVING: 60 kcal, 1 g protein, 3 g fat, 7 g carbohydrates, 0.5 g fiber
SERVING TIP:
For a deeper flavor, lightly toast the almond butter before mixing. This dressing also works well as a drizzle for fruit-based salads or roasted squash.

CITRUS MINT DRESSING

DESCRIPTION:
A bright and invigorating dressing with the sweetness of orange, the tang of lemon, and the refreshing aroma of mint. This dressing is perfect for summer salads, fruit bowls, and light greens, adding a crisp and citrusy finish.
BENEFITS: Rich in vitamin C, refreshing, and mood-boosting.
- **Orange juice** – supports immunity and slows down aging.
- **Mint** – relieves tension and aids digestion.
- **Mustard** – adds a tangy kick.

INGREDIENTS:
- 3 tbsp (45 ml) orange juice
- 1 tbsp (15 ml) lemon juice
- 1 tbsp (15 ml) olive oil
- 1 tsp (5 g) Dijon mustard
- 1 tbsp (5 g) finely chopped fresh mint
- A pinch of salt and freshly ground black pepper

COOKING TIME: 5 minutes
INSTRUCTIONS:
1. In a small bowl or jar, whisk together the orange juice, lemon juice, olive oil, and Dijon mustard.
2. Stir in the chopped mint, salt, and black pepper.
3. Let the dressing sit for 5 minutes to allow the flavors to meld before serving.

NUTRITIONAL VALUE (PER 100 G): 80 kcal, 0.5 g protein, 6 g fat, 7 g carbohydrates, 0.3 g fiber
NUTRITIONAL VALUE PER SERVING: 40 kcal, 0.25 g protein, 3 g fat, 3.5 g carbohydrates, 0.15 g fiber
SERVING TIP:
For an extra layer of flavor, add a pinch of grated orange zest or a few drops of balsamic vinegar. This dressing also works beautifully as a light marinade for grilled vegetables.

HONEY MUSTARD BALSAMIC DRESSING

DESCRIPTION:
A rich and tangy dressing with the perfect balance of sweetness from honey, the boldness of Dijon mustard, and the deep complexity of balsamic vinegar. This dressing pairs well with leafy greens, roasted vegetables, and warm grain salads, adding depth and a hint of sweetness.
BENEFITS: Warming, boosts metabolism and supports vascular health.
- **Mustard** – accelerates metabolism.
- **Honey** – a natural source of energy.
- **Balsamic vinegar** – aids digestion.

INGREDIENTS:
- 2 tbsp (30 ml) olive oil
- 1 tbsp (15 ml) balsamic vinegar
- 1 tsp (5 ml) Dijon mustard
- 1 tsp (5 ml) honey
- A pinch of salt and freshly ground black pepper

COOKING TIME: 5 minutes
INSTRUCTIONS:
1. In a small bowl or jar, combine all ingredients.
2. Whisk or shake vigorously until well blended.
3. Let sit for 5 minutes before serving to allow the flavors to develop.

NUTRITIONAL VALUE (PER 100 G): 110 kcal, 0.3 g protein, 11 g fat, 3 g carbohydrates, 0 g fiber
NUTRITIONAL VALUE PER SERVING: 55 kcal, 0.15 g protein, 5.5 g fat, 1.5 g carbohydrates, 0 g fiber
SERVING TIP:
For an extra layer of flavor, add a pinch of crushed garlic or a few drops of lemon juice. This dressing also works well as a glaze for roasted vegetables or grilled tofu.

SPINACH GARLIC DRESSING

DESCRIPTION:
A vibrant green dressing packed with the earthy freshness of spinach and the bold aroma of garlic. This dressing is perfect for hearty salads, grilled vegetables, and roasted potatoes, adding a rich, savory depth and a burst of nutrients.
BENEFITS: Supports detoxification.
- **Spinach** – a source of iron and B vitamins.
- **Garlic** – a natural antibiotic that strengthens immunity.
- **Lemon** – enhances iron absorption.

INGREDIENTS:
- 1 cup (30 g) fresh spinach leaves
- 1 garlic clove, minced
- 3 tbsp (45 ml) olive oil
- 1 tbsp (15 ml) lemon juice
- A pinch of salt

COOKING TIME: 5 minutes
INSTRUCTIONS:
1. In a blender or food processor, combine spinach, garlic, olive oil, lemon juice, and salt.
2. Blend until smooth and creamy. If the dressing is too thick, add a teaspoon of water to adjust consistency.
3. Use immediately or store in the refrigerator for up to 2 days.

NUTRITIONAL VALUE (PER 100 G): 95 kcal, 1.5 g protein, 9 g fat, 2 g carbohydrates, 0.8 g fiber
NUTRITIONAL VALUE PER SERVING: 47 kcal, 0.75 g protein, 4.5 g fat, 1 g carbohydrates, 0.4 g fiber
SERVING TIP:
For a spicier kick, add a pinch of red pepper flakes. This dressing also works beautifully as a drizzle over grilled chicken or fish.

SPINACH GARLIC DRESSING

DESCRIPTION:
A vibrant green dressing packed with the earthy freshness of spinach and the bold aroma of garlic. This dressing is perfect for hearty salads, grilled vegetables, and roasted potatoes, adding a rich, savory depth and a burst of nutrients.
BENEFITS: Powerful anti-inflammatory effects.
- **Ginger** – boosts metabolism.
- **Turmeric** – neutralizes free radicals.
- **Olive oil** – enhances turmeric absorption.

INGREDIENTS:
- 1 cup (30 g) fresh spinach leaves
- 1 garlic clove, minced
- 3 tbsp (45 ml) olive oil
- 1 tbsp (15 ml) lemon juice
- A pinch of salt

COOKING TIME: 5 minutes
INSTRUCTIONS:
1. In a blender or food processor, combine spinach, garlic, olive oil, lemon juice, and salt.
2. Blend until smooth and creamy. If the dressing is too thick, add a teaspoon of water to adjust consistency.
3. Use immediately or store in the refrigerator for up to 2 days.

NUTRITIONAL VALUE (PER 100 G): 95 kcal, 1.5 g protein, 9 g fat, 2 g carbohydrates, 0.8 g fiber
NUTRITIONAL VALUE PER SERVING: 47 kcal, 0.75 g protein, 4.5 g fat, 1 g carbohydrates, 0.4 g fiber
SERVING TIP:
For a spicier kick, add a pinch of red pepper flakes. This dressing also works beautifully as a drizzle over grilled chicken or fish.

CONCLUSION

Dear Reader,

Our journey into the world of magical salads has come to an end. This book is not just a collection of recipes; it is your guide to the art of balancing flavors, textures, and aromas. It reveals the magic in every ingredient, inspiring creativity and care for yourself and your loved ones.

By preparing these dishes, you give yourself more than just a delicious meal. You nourish your body with essential nutrients, delight your taste buds, and create an atmosphere of harmony with nature. Seasonal ingredients, the foundation of this book, remind us of the importance of staying in tune with the natural rhythm of life and the abundance of beauty and benefits that every season offers.

THE MAGIC IS IN THE DETAILS

Every salad you create is a small culinary masterpiece. It can be light and fresh like a spring breeze, hearty and warming like an autumn sunset, or bright and festive like a winter wonderland.

Don't be afraid to experiment! Magic happens when we allow ourselves to be creative: adding favorite spices, trying new combinations, or decorating dishes as your imagination suggests. Let your own "spells" in the kitchen be not only delicious but also unforgettable.

GRATITUDE

I sincerely thank you for choosing this book. You have become a part of its magical story. I hope the recipes, tips, and tricks within these pages have not only made your meals tastier and healthier but also added a touch of magic to your everyday life. If this book inspired you to experiment in the kitchen, if its recipes brightened your table and brought joy, please share your impressions! I'd love to see your reviews and photos of the dishes you've made. Each of your responses is a contribution to the ongoing magic we create together.

https://www.amazon.com/review/create-review/?ie=UTF8&channel=glance-detail&asin=B0DWFHH53Y

UNTIL WE MEET AGAIN

This is just the beginning of a magical journey. Ahead lie new books, new recipes, and new adventures in the kitchen. Thank you for being here, for your trust, and for the inspiration you bring.

With warmth and sincerity,
Michael Rivers

Transformative Nutrition: Comprehensive Guides to Healthy Eating, Weight Loss, and Sustainable Wellness

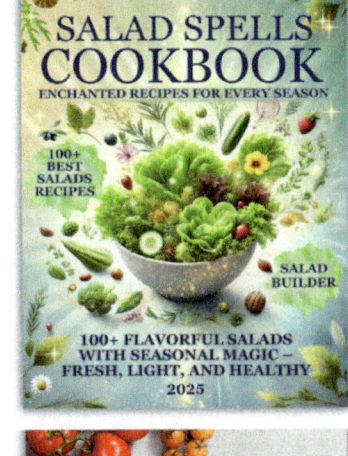

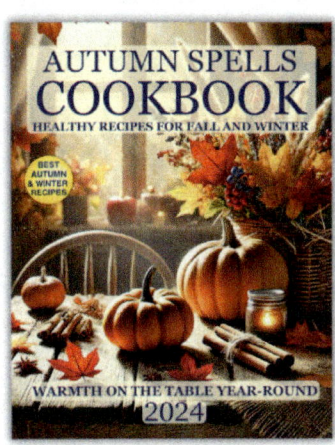

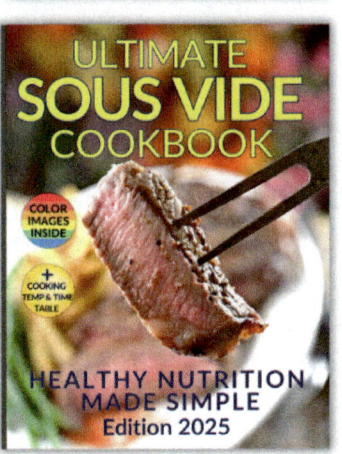

Find more books on the page here

Printed in Great Britain
by Amazon